‹SKYSTRUCK›

True Tales of an Alaska Bush Pilot

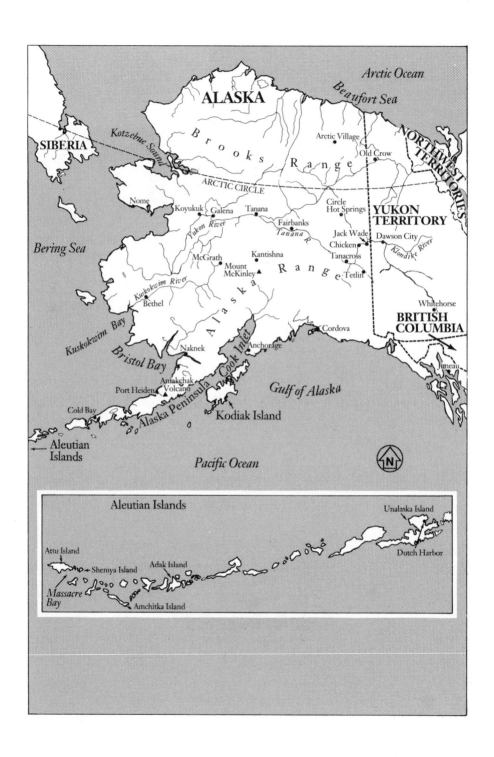

·SKYSTRUCK·

True Tales of an Alaska Bush Pilot

BY

HERMAN LERDAHL

WITH

CLIFF CERNICK

Alaska Northwest Books™
Anchorage • Seattle

Second printing 1990

Library of Congress Cataloging-in-Publication Data
Lerdahl, Herman, 1906–1983.
Skystruck : the life of an Alaska bush pilot / by Herman Lerdahl with Cliff Cernick.
p.   cm.
ISBN 0-88240-356-7
1. Lerdahl, Herman, 1906–1983. 2. Bush pilots–Alaska–Biography.
I. Cernick, Cliff, 1918– . II. Title.
TL540.L42A3 1987   629.13'092–dc20   [B]   89-33729   CIP

Edited by Ethel Dassow and Ellen Harkins Wheat
Book Design by Doug Deay
Cover illustration by Nancy Gellos
Cartography by Karen G. Smith
All photographs are courtesy of Daisy Lerdahl unless otherwise noted.

Alaska Northwest Books™
A division of GTE Discovery Publications, Inc.
22026 20th Ave. S.E.
Bothell, WA 98021

Printed in U.S.A.

To Daisy Lerdahl

CONTENTS

PREFACE

LEVERETT G. RICHARDS, aviation editor of the Portland *Oregonian*, commented on one of his writing trips to Alaska in 1949: "Alaska is full of pilots who make Paul Bunyan look like Little Lord Fauntleroy."

Herm Lerdahl was one of those pilots. He was one of the most remarkable men who ever flew in Alaska or anywhere else for that matter. He was a man who needed to fly, it seems, with almost a primal urgency. On the ground, he felt restless and unfulfilled. His most forlorn moments were those when circumstances kept him earth-bound. Only when he was flying was he able to revel in a world of challenge and excitement.

Flying, for Lerdahl, became a dynamic, driving irresistible force. In the depths of the Great Depression, destiny brought Alaska aviation pioneer Noel Wien to the little Mesabi town of Virginia, Minnesota, where Herm pumped gas for a living. From that moment, he was inescapably bound to the sky. He was to fly more than 5,500 hours in the Alaska bush.

Flying came to Lerdahl as naturally as inventiveness did to Edison, as ballet did to Baryshnikov; there is no other explanation for the sheer magnificence of his performance aloft. His was a consummate skill in a complex environment. Invariably, whether he was cheating death by landing on a helter-skelter Alaska construction site, the perilous slope of a treacherous snow-swept volcano, or a remote winding river at midnight, his matchless command of the sky prevailed.

Lerdahl was tough, but his toughness stemmed from his struggle to survive in the harsh environment of early-day Alaska. He was also a compassionate and caring person — a man who didn't hesitate, for example, to risk his own life to rescue a sourdough who otherwise would have perished in the wilderness. There were many such incidents in his career.

Lerdahl deeply loved Alaska and found immense satisfaction in being able to link prospectors, trappers, hunters and traders, through flying, with the "outside world." At a time when virulent prejudice had infected some sections of Alaska, Lerdahl demonstrated his admiration and respect for Alaska's Natives in countless ways. And the Natives reciprocated by turning out en masse when he flew to the villages bringing mail and supplies. They appreciated him for his seemingly effortless mastery of the sky and for connecting them with the wonders of the white man's world.

Lerdahl was the first Alaskan pilot hired by the Morrison-Knudsen Construction Company in the frantic pre-Pearl Harbor days when an ill-prepared Territory was bracing for an invasion by the Japanese and defense construction was proceeding at a feverish pace. He went on to challenge what has been called "the worst weather in the world" as a captain for Northwest Airlines, bringing mail and supplies to troops on the Aleutian Chain — all without a single fatality or any serious damage to the aircraft he flew.

The exploits in this book are Herm Lerdahl's, and to a large extent so are many of the word-for-word descriptions of those exploits. My role was largely one of editing and reorganizing the voluminous mass of material made available to me by his wife, Daisy, in an attempt to bring the remarkable Lerdahl saga vividly to life. Throughout this process, I did my best to remain true to the spirit of Herm's life embodied in his detailed manuscripts, diaries, logs, and notes. Occasionally, I found it necessary to incorporate additional material from my own research, but I tried to keep such insertions to a minimum. So what you are about to read is the real Lerdahl.

If, through this book, I have been able to help carve out the niche Herm Lerdahl so richly deserves in Alaska aviation history alongside such immortals as Noel Wien, Ray Petersen, Bob Reeve and Jack Jefford, then the seemingly endless hours I devoted to *Skystruck* have been well spent.

Cliff Cernick
Public Affairs Officer (Retired)
Federal Aviation Administration, Alaska Region
Anchorage
May 30, 1989

1

ALASKA AT LAST

IN THE WINTER of 1934 my brother Ed, who owned a Fairbanks garage, wrote that there just might be an opportunity up North for a guy with 218 hours of flying time and a hitherto unused commercial license.

Now, on a bitterly cold January day in 1935 — exactly five years since Noel Wien had kindled flying fire in me back in Minnesota — I was trudging down an Alaska Steamship Company gangway at Valdez in a howling blizzard.

The bitter blasts of powdery snow stinging my face instantly chilled any daydreams I might have had about an adventurous bush-flying career in Alaska. Ed assured me he'd help me repair the two old planes he'd scrounged up somehow — a Stinson and a Monocoupe — and then I'd be on my way. Now, with just fifty-five dollars between me and starvation, I felt cornered. Repairing Ed's beat-up planes, I knew, would take rather than make cash. I knew I had one hell of a struggle on my hands.

As I reached the dock, I was startled to hear my name being called by a man in a sealskin parka.

"Herm Lerdahl!" he called as he broke away from the dock-side crowd and began angling toward me. "Herm!"

Though Ed had assured me someone would meet me, I didn't dream it would be Noel Wien himself. I hadn't seen Noel since we'd met briefly back in Minnesota five years ago. Now, strangely, I recognized him instantly as I grabbed his outstretched hand.

"Welcome to the frozen North, Herm," he said.

1

"Real good to see you again, Noel," I told him.

After some small talk, we bent into the stinging wind and made our way through a narrow snow canyon carved out in front of weather-beaten buildings resembling Western movie false fronts.

In the hotel lobby, old-timers in chairs along the wall studied us curiously.

"Breakfast at seven," Noel said as I scrawled my name in the yellowed register. "We've got lots to talk about, but we're both bushed now."

In my room, exhausted from the long voyage, I shucked my clothes quickly and hit the sack. Sleep eluded me, though, and all kinds of thoughts crowded in as I lay drowsily watching curtains of snow whip across the windowpane, and hearing the faint moan of wind sweeping along the eaves.

Half awake and half asleep, my thoughts drifted back to the day Noel Wien had arrived in Virginia, Minnesota — the most important day in my life up to that time. He was returning to Alaska with his newly purchased orange-and-black Stinson J-5-9. After beelining across the Great Lakes from Detroit, he touched down to refuel at our little airport near the Mesabi iron range.

Though I wasn't aware of it at the time, Wien had already distinguished himself in Alaska aviation. By the time I met him he had become the first man to fly commercially from Fairbanks to Nome, and the first to fly from Alaska to Siberia. Even then, he was laying the groundwork for what would become Alaska's largest intrastate carrier.

Minnesota-born Wien began flying in 1921 and came North in 1924 to take a bush-flying job offered by Jimmy Rodebaugh, a Fairbanks businessman. He brought with him his World War I Standard J-1. He and his mechanic, Bill Yunker, reassembled the flimsy craft at the large public park which also served as Anchorage's first airfield. On the Fourth of July, Wien treated Anchorage residents to almost an hour of Midwest-style barnstorming — loops, wingovers and tailspins. Then he briskly began selling "joy hops" to more than 170 adventurous onlookers, few of whom had ever flown before. The air taxi jaunts continued well into the long twilight of the Midnight Sun.

Bolstered by the payoff of his first Alaska business venture, the twenty-five-year-old Wien departed for Fairbanks, tracing the right-of-way of the Alaska Railroad and, incidentally, establishing another record — the first nonstop flight from Anchorage to Fairbanks.

For me, Wien's arrival in Virginia, Minnesota, in 1929 was a major event. All fired up by word that an airplane had arrived, I sped to the airport in my old Chevy.

Just the sight of his brightly painted plane, sleek and shiny like a huge dragonfly poised for flight, filled me with wonder. I circled it several times, gaping at it from all angles, then pressed my face tight against the windshield, feeling a kind of shiver as I saw the array of dials, knobs and levers.

Noel Wien walked up alongside.

"You a pilot?" he asked.

"Not yet," I said. "I run a gas station here. Name's Herm Lerdahl."

The stocky, powerfully built man, with an even-featured, weather-tanned face, stretched out a grease-stained hand. "Noel Wien," he said. "From Fairbanks, Alaska."

"Any chance of hitching a ride, Mr. Wien?"

He brightened instantly. "Costs fifteen bucks an hour to operate," he informed me. "If you and two other guys can scrape up five bucks each, well, I'll give you a ride you'll never forget."

I began sprinting toward my car even before he finished. "Don't go anywhere!" I yelled. I was back in less than fifteen minutes with two buddies, Harold and Ed Johnson, who brought the contents of their piggy banks.

Wien carefully counted the fares, then told the Johnsons, "You fellas crawl in back, and be careful of the upholstery. Herm, you ride up front with me — you're my co-pilot."

I cinched my seat belt tight, watching the prop's blurred circle dissolve into invisibility, my heart pounding at the engine's mounting roar and the accelerating surge of the ground sweeping away beneath us. Numb with undreamed-of excitement, I stared at the constricting world below, the transformed, toy-sized villages of Eveleth and Gilbert and the mere pothole that was the giant Mesabi depression. How can I express it? A kind of fever took possession of me there high over Minnesota, as I was suspended in a boundless world of vast distances, far horizons and maplike topography, in a new, exciting, zestful dimension I had never known existed. It was a fever that was to rage within me for the rest of my life.

3

All too soon, Wien was banking and heading back, skillfully guiding the plane down a precisely tilted air pathway that merged with the runway's threshold. The flight left me in wordless trance, a swimmer splashing happily in a river that surged with all kinds of emotions and feelings, swept away with the current that was flying.

I saw Wien studying me as we taxied up to the edge of the field. He must have known, because he was grinning and maybe remembering the way it was when he first flew.

"Well, Herm?"

I kept squinting at the dirty gray of the late afternoon sky where a winter storm was brewing, and searched for words to express what had happened to me. Hooked. Skystruck. Sky-dazed. It was almost too much and I kept gulping.

"No comment?" he asked.

"Yeah," I said. "Yeah. One of these days . . ."

Wien thumped me approvingly on the shoulder. "You'll never regret it," he said.

In the months ahead I threw myself almost recklessly into the struggle to become a pilot, working long hours at my dead-end gas station job to eke out the money flying lessons gobbled up. But when no flying jobs developed after I got my commercial license, I had to fight off feelings of disillusion. I still loved flying as fervently as ever but, with the whole country in a depression, what was I going to do with my "ticket"?

Ed's letter, suggesting that I might want to come to Alaska and try my luck at bush flying, came at a time when I was close to rock bottom, not knowing where to turn in pursuit of my dream of flying for a living.

Now, as the blizzard raged outside my hotel room in snow-bound Valdez, I began drifting off. What the heck, I thought, as sleep began taking over. I'm in Alaska — a big, new country made just for pilots. Maybe . . . just maybe.

The next morning at breakfast, I got Dutch-uncle talk on Alaska flying from Wien.

"Those of us still busting our butts flying up here know one thing for sure," he commented as he glanced idly at the storm still raging outside. "Bush flying is a tough, thankless business and unless you're tough yourself, you can take one hell of a pounding. The damn business will slam you up against the ropes again and again. If you belong in Alaska you'll stay in there and fight. If you don't, you'll throw in the towel.

"If you're going to stay alive as a pilot up here, Herm, there's one thing you've got to remember: respect the weather. Never play Russian roulette with the weather — sometimes, every chamber is loaded. Never let anyone talk you into flying somewhere against your best judgment. When the weather's lousy and some jerk insists he's just got to get there, back off. Be tough as nails. Learn to say no and mean it. If they threaten to get someone else to fly them where you won't, just say, 'That's up to you.' You'll find, in the long run, that they'll respect you for being stubborn about risking people's necks." The bush-flying wisdom Wien shared with me, then and later, helped guide me through some rugged flying situations in the years ahead, and I've always been grateful to him for it.

The next morning dawned bright and clear, lifting the curtain on a world of shimmering, rose-tinted mountains that plunged sharply into the sea. High on the ridges, fierce winds blew thin veils of powdery snow across shadowed valleys embroidered with frozen waterfalls. A Minnesota flatlander, unused to such displays, I felt like bowing my head.

Up and down Main Street, bundled-up Valdez residents were digging away at flowing, wind-carved dunes. By the time we got to the airport, a bulldozer had gouged out a narrow departure corridor not much wider than wingtip-to-wingtip. Wien performed a thundering, ruler-straight, unswerving takeoff out of this ticklish snow canyon.

As Wien's six-place Bellanca banked smoothly over Valdez and headed north, I began to get a pilot's-eye view of the vastness of Alaska. There was an overwhelming intensity about the parade of lakes, rivers and glaciers that began to unfold. It was as if the land, from horizon to horizon, was singing and proclaiming and calling out in language that was strangely foreign yet able to penetrate a man's soul. Everything I saw seemed haunting, and I began to understand what Robert Service was writing about when he spoke of "a land that beckons."

By the time we reached Fairbanks, murky twilight had merged into inky blackness. Suddenly, the northern sky burst into shimmering, dancing tendrils and sprays of color. What a welcome!

With hardly a jolt, the plane's gear merged with the frozen

runway. As we came to a smooth halt, the flying maestro in the left seat turned to me with a grin. "We're home, Herm," he said.

2

UNFORGETTABLE CHARTERS

FAIRBANKS, WHEN I FIRST SAW IT in 1935, was a raw gold-mining town half hidden by dismal ice fog. The main street was peppered with honky-tonks, and in the red-light district near the post office, gaudily painted sporting women beckoned to sex-starved men from the camps and creeks. To frustrated, lonely working men, the bright lights of Fairbanks must have seemed like a glittering oasis of pleasure in a bleak and bitter world.

Why any rational person would choose to settle down in such a godforsaken place was a mystery to me until I got to know the people. I remember them as one big, happy family who showed genuine concern and regard for one another and were ready to help each other in any way. Once Fairbanks accepted you, the community's warmth embraced and bolstered you.

My brother Ed came to town five years before I did, broke like me. A skilled mechanic, he managed to open one of the town's first garages. Ed and his wife, Bea, lived in a large cabin on a big lot near the post office. Though struggling to stay afloat himself, Ed did what he could to get me started in a town that was filled with the unemployed and needy.

A pilot himself, Ed had acquired the remains of a two-place 90-horsepower Monocoupe that had crashed about ten miles south of town. Later he had picked up a badly smashed Stinson SM-8A and hauled it to his ramshackle hangar at the airport. A fire that razed his hangar destroyed the Monocoupe but spared the wreckage of the Stinson parked outside. Ed figured we would be able to resurrect the

Stinson. I had my doubts and could only shake my head when I saw the ugly, ice-coated carcass.

Ed and I had driven to the hangar ruins with Dick Ortman, a crackerjack Pan Am mechanic, who studied the wreck carefully. With the toe of his ice-coated boot, he gingerly lifted the shattered tail section to get a look at the twisted underside. All I saw was jagged metal and ripped fabric; Dick saw possibilities.

"Have 'er in the air in less'n three months," he announced.

You're crazy, I thought. In less than the promised three months Dick's wizardry transformed that heap of junk into a proud silver bird.

The work I saw Dick and other mechanics do would never cease to amaze me. The breed of aviation mechanics I came to know displayed remarkable ingenuity and dedication. There should be a Hall of Fame somewhere to honor pioneer mechanics like Ernie Hubbard, Ray Pratt, Fritz Wien, Bob Clemens, Warren Tillman, Eddie Moore, Charles Fideles and others.

Fideles, for example, just loved being around planes. I sensed his devotion every time I saw him stroll past a plane. He was gifted with the knack of "instant invention." He could quickly conjure up a gadget or part needed to solve a nagging problem. Another "instant inventor" was Ernie Hubbard, Wien's shop foreman, who devised a marvelous hot-air scoop that kept the carburetor from freezing. It was far superior to anything manufactured.

On May 1, 1935, I did more than thirty test takeoffs and landings in Ed's resurrected Stinson. It performed flawlessly. I was delighted to be flying again and began diligently schooling myself in short takeoffs and landings to prepare for abbreviated bush fields. Soon I was able to get in and out of 600-foot-long bush strips with no sweat.

Working out of Ed's tiny garage-office, where Ed's wife handled the accounts, the sole pilot of the Lerdahl Flying Service was now ready for business. Day after day, full of determination, I canvassed the town's hotels and rooming houses for business. There wasn't any until May 12, when I snagged my first charter — hauling supplies to the Krager gold operation at No Grub Creek, ninety miles east of Fairbanks.

No Grub Creek's thousand-foot, boulder-strewn strip was a real challenge. Two lines of tall trees bracketed the field like giant green bookends. Getting off the field was just as thrilling as getting on.

Over the next few months I began regular flights to such places as Koyukuk, Nulato, Nome, Golovin, Wiseman, Copper Center, Circle Hot Springs and Valdez.

Too much of my business in those early months was on credit, and when customers didn't pay, I really suffered. Bush flying in the early '30s was a grim struggle for survival. We fought tooth and nail for any business there was. "Body-snatchers" — pilots who "stole" your passengers and cargo — abounded. I got stung by one of these villains when I flew an old sourdough to his gold claims at Chicken, near the Alaska-Canada border. At our destination, the husky, long-bearded passenger had just wrestled his packsack out of the Stinson and was trudging toward his log cabin when another prospector wanting to fly back to town asked about the fare. We settled on forty bucks. I detoured briefly to nearby bushes to relieve myself. By the time I returned, my passenger had vanished — "body-snatched." He was aboard a plane I saw taking off. There are times when a grown man feels like bawling. Those forty lost dollars loomed awfully big to me then. I flew back feeling betrayed and robbed. From then on, I kept closer watch on passengers.

■ ■ ■

A few of my early charter trips were memorable. I've never forgotten, for example, the stupendous chewing-out I got from Bill Lavery. With his parents, Bill operated the largest grocery store in Fairbanks. Being just short of getting his commercial license, Bill chartered me to fly a load of freight to Kantishna in his Standard, a five-place open cockpit biplane. I had never flown there before, and after what happened I had no desire to return.

Lavery stuffed the plane with so much cargo that he was forced to abandon the right seat. He had to spread-eagle himself across the ceiling-high heap of supplies in the back, something not recommended by the Civil Aeronautics Authority.

Lavery's nine-cylinder Standard with its wide, beautifully tapered wing was a joy to fly. Soaring high over the tundra, I lolled back totally relaxed, hands off the controls, occasionally applying gentle rudder pressure to keep my course.

Relaxation ended abruptly when we entered the narrow

canyon leading to the mine. Here, towering granite outcrops, like huge gray boxes stacked in disarray, forced me to fly in slalom fashion. At our destination, the "nice, long sandbar" Bill assured me was there turned out to be nothing short of hair-raising for a new bush pilot. The landing area tilted steeply downhill from the approach end. This would produce far greater landing speed than I wanted. Still worse, the opposite end of the runway plunged abruptly into a boiling glacial river. Because of the terrain, no go-around was possible, so you had to get in the first time without a hitch.

I managed to touch down precisely on the first yard of the "top-of-the-hill" strip. Then everything went wrong. The overload greased the downhill speed, quickly gobbling up our precious landing area and bringing the disastrous drop-off zooming toward me alarmingly. I was forced to jam on the brakes, with expected results. The lighter section of the aircraft — the tail — slowly arced upward until it was vertical and then the plane toppled over. We were on our back right at the rim of the drop-off.

As we were overturning, Lavery released a streak of mule-skinner cussing with rare virtuosity.

"You put us on our back, you son of a bitch," he raged. Though the bulk of the cargo pinned him down, Lavery's cussing continued to a crescendo, which delighted me because it told me he was still all right. I opened the door and somehow he managed to scramble out on the rocks without missing a red-hot beat.

I had never heard so magnificent a tirade delivered with such fervor for so long. I had to admire the flair with which he chewed me out, and it wasn't the least bit annoying, strangely. Those verbal fireballs danced off me like hail off a roof. I was thoroughly disgusted with myself, and nothing Bill could say could make me feel worse. Besides, a guy who treasured his aircraft and lavished on it all his extra cash and spare time needed a steam valve at a time like this.

After I crawled out I began carefully inspecting the plane, even though the volcano was still erupting. The Standard was resting on its top cylinders and wingtips. Incredibly, except for a tiny dent in the rudder, there didn't seem to be the slightest damage.

After supper, camp workers with ropes set the plane right side up and unloaded the cargo. I checked the controls and was relieved to find that they functioned perfectly.

By now, Vesuvius had become dormant. Lavery was

beginning to feel better and look somewhat sheepish. He took over as pilot for the flight back to gain flying time toward the two hundred hours he needed for his commercial. Once free of the treacherous canyon, Bill tried to make amends.

"Imagine putting a plane over on its back and just denting the rudder," he began. "Damn lucky."

Except for a faint "uh-huh," I kept my mouth shut.

He tried again. "Herm, I know you did absolutely everything you could to avoid what happened back there. I want you to know . . ."

"Look, Bill," I interrupted, "it's not important. In your shoes I'd probably have felt the same way, though I might have expressed myself differently."

He was at ease again, knowing his unspoken apology had been accepted. We both grinned.

I never held Bill Lavery's tirade against him. Even so, I couldn't help wondering where a nice, well-brought-up, clean-cut guy like Bill Lavery had picked up such a raunchy vocabulary.

Stark terror rode with me on October 12, 1937, the day I flew a college professor, Earl Pilgrim, to his claims on the Kantishna. Pilgrim was one of the first six professors at the University of Alaska. He began teaching in 1922, when the university had six students and six teachers. His mine in the Kantishna Mining District was at Stampede Creek.

On that Kantishna trip I learned that once a pilot lets himself get trapped in a blind canyon in conditions of poor visibility, they might as well prepare his obituary. I was unquestionably doomed. The fact that I escaped has to be attributed to incredible luck.

Flying up Alaska's blind canyons has snuffed out the lives of numerous pilots. Through carelessness, they become hopelessly sandwiched between unyielding perpendicular rock walls too narrow to allow them to turn around. All they can do is attempt to climb out. Disaster is almost inevitable because Alaska's grim canyons are noted for climbing faster than virtually any type of aircraft can. On that day, I knew the kind of fright that paralyzes a pilot as he struggles desperately to elude a canyon's "dead end."

It was twenty below when we took off in the Stinson toward Mount McKinley with four hundred pounds of cargo, then veered off to follow the Kantishna River that bores through sheer rock walls. It was my first experience at being fenced in on both sides. As light snow began to fall and visibility plunged to less than two miles, my apprehension grew.

"We're almost there," Pilgrim assured me, but I felt the touch of fear.

"How far now, Earl?" I asked nervously as my eyes strained to spot the elusive landing area.

Pilgrim was too busy scrutinizing the snow-shrouded terrain to answer. A few moments later he yelled jubilantly, "There! To your right!"

I got a fleeting glimpse of the tiny clearing, turned right, and cut the throttle to touch down quickly before visibility got worse.

Pilgrim draped tarps over the four hundred pounds of supplies, which he planned to pack to his cabin about a quarter of a mile from the landing field.

I should have stayed with Pilgrim until the weather cleared, but I was eager to get back, encouraged by a slight improvement in the visibility. But after I had taken off and skimmed the right side of the canyon, the snow curtain dropped again and to my horror the visibility switched to zero-zero. There was no way of telling where the rock walls lurked. I was trapped, trying to fight off waves of panic. My mind frantically sorted the options and settled on the only one left: an attempt at a "blind" climb out of the canyon in upward spirals, with huge tombstones all around.

I poured on full power to begin my desperate climb, feeling caught in a dark, formless void and with no inkling of the boundaries I had to maintain.

Spiraling upward slowly, I welcomed the good, steady hum of the engine. I held the wheel gingerly and prayed I wouldn't spin in.

Then what seemed like a miracle brought a faint bit of hope: the blurred outline of the sun's disk appeared to the left. As long as I had it as a point of reference, I could continue to climb smoothly. The sudden disappearance of the disk sent a kind of paralysis sweeping over me.

I haven't got long now, I told myself. Oh, God, I'm going to hit. Any time now.

Feeling totally helpless, I turned left to what I hoped was forty-five degrees, then straightened out. Suddenly my long-lost friend, the sun disk, reappeared, this time on the right side of the windshield. Seconds slid past with alarming slowness.

I glanced at the altimeter: seven thousand feet and climbing. Getting lighter, I noticed with relief. At seventy-six hundred, I broke out of the gloom into the clear. Looming around me were the awesome pinnacles of jagged peaks, some thrusting as high as nine thousand feet. I was limp with thankfulness at being spared.

As nearly as I could estimate, I had flown totally without visibility for at least seven minutes. Empty, under full power, the Stinson was capable of climbing between seven hundred and eight hundred feet a minute. Throughout that critical time, it functioned flawlessly. Had I stalled even for an instant or made the slightest change in the plane's power or direction, I'm convinced I would have spun in. All this may sound incredible to pilots reading this, but remember, I lived to tell about it.

On February 18, 1938, I flew Bill Oliver, a rugged, six-foot-four outdoorsman who loved roaming Alaska's hills even in winter, to Goodpaster Creek about a hundred miles east of Fairbanks.

We left at noon and soon reached the creek's headwaters, where Oliver wanted to be dropped off. The designated landing spot was a stretch of frozen river bordered by frozen, stunted trees and boxed in by sawtooth peaks.

Circling, I carefully sized up that stretch of river, confident I'd be able to turn around at the end of the 800-foot-long landing area.

Beyond that flat stretch, the river disappeared into a blind canyon guarded by a wicked collection of huge boulders.

My approach and descent were fine. I set down at precisely the right spot on the river, cut the throttle, and expected the drag of the snow cover to get me stopped well ahead of the boulders.

As we skimmed the surface and touched down, Bill started yelling in alarm: "That's not snow we're landing on, Herm, it's glare ice!" Wind had blasted snow off the straight stretch, then freezing weather had coated the glassy surface with a deceptive layer of frost. Now, with next to zero friction on the surface, we were catapulting toward the rock pile, a runaway plane totally out of control. There was little likelihood I could avert a crash. Desperately, I jammed hard left rudder. This swung the tail a bit but did nothing to cut speed, except that now we were barreling toward the rocks a bit askew.

Hard right rudder. Blast of power. The plane turned around 180 degrees but we kept zooming toward the rocks — and disaster — tail first.

In a frantic, last-ditch effort to cancel momentum I kept full power blasting. That did it. Gradually, the engine power brought us to a halt. Only inches remained between the tail and the boulders.

■ ■ ■

My last charter before freeze-up, 1939, was to Wild Lake in the Endicott Mountains, 235 miles northwest of Fairbanks. The crystal-clear, five-mile-long lake resembled a huge, glistening emerald as I touched down on floats.

I was bringing in supplies for the area's only year-round residents, Ed Smith and his native wife, Mary, and Ed's bachelor brother, George. The Smiths mined in the summer and trapped in the winter. Grayling and rainbows teemed in the lake so abundantly that I once caught three fish at the same time with a triple fly.

That evening, Mary served sizzling moose steaks with thick, tasty gravy and golden sourdough biscuits. After dinner we gabbed far into the Arctic night, staying awake until fully talked out.

At bedtime Mary brought out a stuffed duffel bag lined with clean sheets. Between the bed where she and her husband slept and my cot she hung a blanket on a tight line.

On the previous trip, Ed had handed me a poke bulging with nuggets. "Enough there to pay for our supplies and your round trip," he said. "If anything's left just buy us something you think we'd like."

I knew exactly what to buy with the sixty-five dollars left over. The Smiths didn't have a radio so I purchased a Zenith Trans-Oceanic table model shortwave set with a thousand-hour battery.

"Are you sure it'll work way out here so far from the stations?" Mary asked when I delivered the radio.

"Mary," I assured her, "that radio's going to work."

Her dark eyes glowed and her hands clasped as if in prayer. "Oh, I sure hope so," she said.

To insure good reception, I installed a twenty-five-foot section of lead-in wire and a hundred feet of antenna. While Ed and Mary waited in hushed anticipation, I hooked up the battery and switched on the radio.

There was silence for a long moment. Then, the crisp voice of a British announcer filled the room. "This is the BBC in London with today's news," he said.

Mary gasped, and both of them looked absolutely delighted. "You've brought the world to us, Herm, and given us company for the long winter nights."

Six months later, on my next trip to Wild Lake, Mary proudly showed me a lined writing tablet on which she'd recorded every station they'd listened to during the past winter. Included were broadcasts from virtually every country on the globe.

Being able to "bring the world" to Mary and Ed Smith gave me a world of satisfaction.

3

COPING WITH COLD

EVEN MINNESOTA'S bruising winters hadn't prepared me for
the blistering cold of Alaska's Interior and Yukon Territory.

When it got sixty-five below or worse, Wien pilots
stayed put. They dressed for survival. Winter mornings, I'd yank
on heavy wool long johns, wool pants and a heavy wool shirt. I'd
put on three pairs of heavy wool socks, then wrap a strip of
burlap around each sock. After that, I'd wriggle into moosehide mukluks with half-inch insoles. Encased in that fur and wool
cocoon, I'd be warm and comfortable in the most miserable
weather.

That was how I dressed for my flight in the Stinson to Jack
Wade, Chicken and Dawson on January 5, 1936.

It was sixty-three below when I landed at Dawson's tiny
airport near the Klondike River about eight miles east of town. The
Mounties suggested I stay overnight with a farm family in their large
cabin adjacent to the airport. The couple supplemented their
income providing bed-and-board for itinerant pilots.

After a hearty breakfast, I walked to the plane to begin the
early morning warm-up. I scraped frost off the wings, got the fire pot
going, then checked the Taylor thermometer on one of the struts.
Brrh! The mercury had plummeted below the lowest reading —
sixty-five below. How cold was it? I estimated it was at least seventy-
five below.

A couple of Mounties walked over to help me get started,
their breath billowing out in tiny clouds. One of them gasped when

he glanced at the thermometer. "Hit bottom," he said. "Better stick around."

The Mountie used a nail to etch a tiny mark on the thermometer alongside the position of the mercury. "Keep that," he said. "It's got to be some kind of record."

(Later Jack Frost, who, appropriately, worked for the U.S. Weather Bureau in Fairbanks, sent the thermometer to his Washington headquarters. Their official report, one of my prized possessions, declared that at the scratch-point the Dawson temperature was 86.6 below zero.)

As the farmer came hurrying out with a five-gallon can of warm oil, I shut off the plumber's blowtorch I'd been heating the engine with and we poured the oil in.

Properly warmed, Lycoming engines started easily. Not this day. Even under full power it was sluggish. I kicked left rudder, then right, but in that awful cold I couldn't coax it beyond forty miles an hour. After shuttling back and forth within the same ski tracks, I finally got the plane to stagger off the runway.

I babied the cantankerous beast to about forty-five hundred feet and circled, reluctant to depart while it was acting up. At forty-five hundred, it was colder than on the ground and though the throttle was on full, the engine kept slowing perceptibly. In the North, you don't fly cross-country under those conditions unless you're crazy. I had to go back.

"Knew you wouldn't make it," the farmer said. "Too damn cold. Stay another night — it might warm up by tomorrow."

The farmer brought over his fire pot and we spent a couple of hours heating the engine with two fire pots to get the oil out. Otherwise I'd have a busted engine. That bone-chilling job done, we returned to his warm cabin.

Dawson was practically tropical the next morning — only eight below. Now, the engine purred happily all the way back to Fairbanks.

■ ■ ■

Though that Dawson trip was the coldest, a flight I made to a trapper's cabin thirty miles south of Beaver on the Yukon Flats ran a close second. My cargo for Olaf Solvic, an old sourdough, was a hundred solidly frozen loaves of bread. It was seventy-three below when I landed at his little bush strip where he was waiting with his dog team. The intense cold had frosted his Santa Claus beard and the bristles on the dogs' snouts.

"Join me in a cup of coffee, Herm," he invited when we finished unloading.

"Sorry, not this time, Olaf," I apologized. "Got to get back." His face showed his disappointment; out in the bush, lack of human companionship can be as demoralizing as the cold.

Olaf waved as his team began moving toward the cabin on a nearby ridge. The sight of the old sourdough and his malamutes as he headed toward the cabin with smoke billowing from its chimney resembled something you might see on an Alaskan Christmas card. The scene remains imprinted on my mind to this day.

■ ■ ■

In December, January and February, always the coldest months, Fairbanks temperatures would drop to anywhere from thirty-five to fifty below. At Tetlin it got even colder. On one of my trips there in one of Wien's Cessnas, it was sixty-eight below at 7 A.M. and didn't warm to sixty below until 9 A.M.

At Tetlin, I usually stayed overnight with my old friend John Hajdukovich, a pioneer fur-trader. Always an early riser, John had the cabin warm and a hearty breakfast prepared by the time I was dressed.

I fire-potted the engine myself; it was too dangerous to entrust that to anyone else. If a fire started, the airplane would explode into flames.

A pilot has to follow a careful routine in such devastating cold. To bed the ship down for the night, I turned off the gas valve and applied full choke to use up the last few drops of fuel, leaving none in the carburetor to flare up when I used the fire pot the next day. Just before the engine stopped, I'd taxi onto wood blocks to keep the skis free of snow and frost; otherwise, the plane would freeze to the spot. Finally, I'd drain the oil and give it to the musher to take on to the roadhouse to be kept warm through the night.

Winter operations had to be carefully orchestrated. By the time the musher arrived with the oil, passengers had to be aboard and fire-potting completed.

To allow for extra payload, we never carried a battery in the

Cessna in winter. I'd hand-prop the plane to get the engine started, then scoot back into the cockpit. With the engine roaring away on all seven cylinders, I was ready to depart.

Beginning at forty below, air density is such that even a heavily loaded plane literally leaps into the air. At about three thousand feet I'd usually encounter spectacular temperature inversions, sometimes finding myself in a stratum where it was from zero to thirty above after leaving ground temperatures of from forty to sixty below.

■ ■ ■

It can be miserable, even terrifying, to repair an aircraft in the numbing Arctic cold. On one midwinter flight to Alatna above the Arctic Circle, the forward-backward movement of the control stick seemed haywire. I realized with dread I was going to have to repair the plane at fifty below.

After draining the oil, I inspected the control cables, and found that the little pulley in the far aft of the ship was clogged with ice, causing the elevator cable to slip off and go limp.

Villagers provided me with a Yukon stove and a tent to drape over the tail and fuselage while I was working within the fuselage. I needed to work bare-handed inside the fuselage near the empennage assembly, so the area had to be warmed sufficiently to allow me to do the job without gloves.

The warming took three miserable hours, then I squeezed myself as far as I could into the belly and tail. With aching, icy fingers, I began fumbling at the frozen pulley; outside, showers of sparks like those from a Fourth of July sparkler kept erupting from the chimney of the wood stove. I felt panic, knowing that a single spark could ignite the plane, touching off a fireball that would cremate me as I lay trapped and helpless in the fuselage. I prayed that the Natives wouldn't let the stove get too hot or allow sparks to settle on the fabric. My body ached almost unbearably from being wedged into such cramped quarters.

While one of the Natives worked the turnbuckle back and forth up front, I managed to force the cable back around the pulley and adjust for the proper elevator control tension. When I crawled out of that potential death trap, I was trembling.

It was 7 P.M., dark and sixty below when we thankfully

dismantled the tent and I climbed onto a dogsled to be taken to the village.

The Alatna mission was run by two gracious ladies, Miss Hill and Miss Kay, who, depending upon the occasion, served the villagers as teacher, doctor and nurse.

You could stay overnight at either Don Evans's place or Sam Dubin's rooming house and store, a choice that was always made for you by your musher. That night I heard the musher yell to his companion with the other sled, "Take the oil to Dubin's." The pilot always stayed where his oil did.

Like most roadhouse operators, Sam Dubin charged a buck a meal and a buck a bunk, with the pilot supplying his own sleeping bag. Those who could afford it left a tip.

Alaska's roadhouse operators immensely enjoyed putting up pilots so they could catch up on the news and have someone to talk with, though sometimes they didn't let you do much talking.

At virtually all the roadhouses, everything stopped automatically on the dot of 10 P.M. when the Richfield Reporter came on the air from San Francisco. Only when that ritual was complete could conversation or other activity resume.

My "one buck" breakfast the next morning consisted of ham and eggs, toast, a large bowl of canned fruit, and coffee.

Taking off from the Koyukuk River on the return trip, nothing happened when I applied full-forward pressure on the control stick. The tail seemed to want to stay on the ground. I knew instantly what was wrong. In making repairs, I had forgotten to put a twist in the control cable; now it was in reverse, forcing me to work the elevator stick in reverse to get the tail off the ground. When I got back, the situation was promptly and professionally corrected by Wien's shop foreman, Ernie Hubbard.

4

FROZEN EDEN

THOUGH SAM WHITE, the Fairbanks game warden, had his own biplane, a Swallow with a Kinner air-cooled engine, he occasionally chartered me to fly him out on cases, something I thoroughly enjoyed. I got a call from him on March 16, 1936.

"Got word some trappers will be coming down the Yukon soon with some illegal furs," he said. "I want to lie in wait for 'em at a place called Jordan. I'd like to have you fly me there and keep me company till I nab 'em. Can you get away?"

"Sure, Sam," I said.

I touched down on the ice in front of a cluster of cabins.

"We'll be staying with old man Jordan," Sam said. "Hope you don't mind siwashing it for a couple days."

"Not at all," I said.

It was starting to snow as Sam knocked on Jordan's door. It was opened by Jordan, a tall, bearded, rugged-looking guy decked out in a hand-sewn, multicolored beaded shirt, moosehide pants and fur mukluks. His dark-haired wife stood directly behind him, her opal eyes glowing with curiosity.

"Hope you can put us up for a couple nights," Sam said.

Jordan smiled broadly. "Glad to have you," he said, ushering us to a comfortable room in the back of the cabin with its own stove alongside a stack of wood. Double bunks had been built into one corner.

We got a fire going in the oil-drum stove and around suppertime Jordan offered to give us a couple of moose steaks. "You can cook 'em in our kitchen," he said.

Jordan handed Sam a meat saw and led us out to the cache, where Sam sawed off a couple of inch-thick steaks. That night we enjoyed the succulent steaks, which were topped off with a plate of Mrs. Jordan's fresh-baked biscuits.

Until bedtime, the door between our small room and their living quarters was kept open. After supper we all sat together over coffee, yakking. It turned out that both Sam and Jordan were from Maine so Maine talk predominated the rest of the night.

Very early I observed that, although the Jordans had very little, they seemed supremely happy. Jordan seemed to delight in finding ways to please and compliment his shy wife.

"I've got me an absolute jewel — the best little gal in the world," he told us. "Never could've found anybody like her in Maine. Every day I thank my lucky stars she's mine." He wrapped a burly arm around the slender woman's waist and pulled her close.

"We was both real lucky," said Mrs. Jordan.

Jordan kept praising her despite her apparent embarrassment. "Don't need to go to heaven," he said. "My heaven's right here."

"You two ever fight?" Sam asked mischievously.

"Never," Jordan insisted. "I'd be afraid she'd leave me. Then I'd have to go out and shoot myself.

"Let me tell you how this little girl and I go moose hunting," he continued eagerly. "When our cache is almost empty, we hitch our dog team, load up our gear and mush into the hills. When we run into a nice young bull, I knock it down. In no time she has it skinned. I cut up the meat and we lug the chunks to the sled, throw in the hide, and start back with food for a couple more months."

They were an absolutely wonderful couple, this happy Native-white pair. It seemed that they had discovered their own frozen Eden alongside the Yukon, enjoying to the fullest Alaska's bounty. Though I'm sure life was far from easy for them, having each other seemed to make up for it.

On the third morning Sam was brewing coffee when the crisp, clear Yukon air brought us voices and the sound of yelping dogs.

"That's them for sure," Sam shouted, grabbing his parka. "Nobody else would be coming downriver this time of day."

Through the window we saw two long, dark smudges approaching. Sam rushed out to meet them and confiscated two sledloads of illegally caught, out-of-season furs.

He informed the crestfallen Native lads they had to appear in court in Tanana.

I was all set to go when Sam was ready to leave.

I didn't fly with Sam White for a few months, but I thought of him in October 1936, while returning from a mail trip to Chandalar in an old Fairchild 71 on floats. I wanted to share with him something I'd seen on that trip.

At about four in the afternoon, I was over Beaver Creek south of Fort Yukon when the entire landscape to the south seemed to burst into life. As I soared closer, I saw a slow-moving torrent of caribou flowing across the land. The mighty stream of animals was at least twenty miles wide and thirty miles long. In the fading twilight of that beautiful autumn day, thousands — maybe several hundreds of thousands — of the great animals were surging over the tundra in a great, gray tide.

"Biggest damn caribou migration I've ever seen," I told Sam when I got back to town. "You've got to fly out and see it."

"I'll go over 'em in my Swallow tomorrow at daybreak," he said.

The next day, after flying over the herd, Sam visited me at the hangar. "Hard to believe there's that many caribou in Alaska," he said. "Didn't seem any end to 'em. That's how caribou migrations must have looked before the white man came to Alaska. Will we ever see anything like it again?"

A few days later, Sam again flew over the area where he'd spotted the vast herd.

"Gone," he said. "Broken up. Scattered, split into hundreds of straggling clusters. The wolves were feasting."

Years later, Sam reminded me again of that caribou migration. "Used to be millions of 'em in Alaska," he remarked. "Tremendous herds, bigger than the one we saw. Now they're gone. Just a couple thousand animals left and the herds keep dwindling every year."

"Why, Sam?"

"Damn if I know," he said. "It's puzzled game experts for years — they just don't know why the herds are fading away. Wolves? Over-hunting? Over-grazing? Nobody really knows."

Now that I'm retired, I sometimes loll back in my easy chair, eyes closed, and once again I'm flying over Beaver Creek at four in the afternoon in October 1936. Once again I see that mighty, slow-moving stream of animals.

And I think, too, of those wonderful Jordans, the burly Scandinavian "Adam" and his pretty Native "Eve" who found their Eden on the banks of the Yukon.

5

A SKY FULL OF WINGS

DR. CARTER'S DOG was a sleek, glistening black Labrador with glowing onyx eyes and a heart so flooded with joy at seeing the abundance of waterfowl at Minto Lake that he pirouetted like a ballerina on the lakeshore.

This remarkable animal was the trembling, cavorting, gyrating centerpiece of the three-man hunting party I flew to Minto Lake on September 8, 1940.

Besides Dr. Carter, the party consisted of Ed Clausen, manager of the Fairbanks branch of the Northern Commercial Company, and Major Dale Gaffney, commanding officer of the Air Force's Cold Weather Base at Ladd Field.

The day we flew to the lake, I clashed with Gaffney, a longtime pilot with a distinguished military record.

About half an hour before Dr. Carter arrived with his dog, Gaffney and a party of five GIs roared up to the landing in a GI truck loaded high with supplies. To my dismay, the soldiers began unloading a tent, picnic tables, folding chairs, strings of decoys and several large boxes of grub.

After surveying the operation coldly, I sauntered over.

"We can't take all that stuff," I told Gaffney bluntly.

His face took on a bulldog expression. "Who in hell says we can't?" he demanded, pushing his face close to mine.

"I say so," I said. "I'm the pilot and I decide what we take and what we leave. Clausen's bringing the grub. Those tables and chairs aren't going. Nothing's going except your ammo and your float cushions."

"What about the goddamn decoys?" he barked.

"You won't need any goddamn decoys. There's so many ducks and geese at Minto Lake all you need to do is stand there and shoot. It would be stupid to fly decoys out there."

Painfully conscious of the eavesdropping airmen who were obviously enjoying seeing a civilian challenging the brass, Gaffney thrust his crab-red face close to mine.

"Lerdahl," he snarled, "if you're lying to me, so help me I'm going to kick your goddamn teeth out." Then he peevishly ordered the GIs to reload the stuff.

Clausen arrived at four with a sleeping bag, a duffel bag, a small camp stove, a lantern and several boxes of food. Dr. Carter had only his bedroll, his gun and his hunt-happy dog.

We began loading the Fairchild 71 on floats for the fifty-mile flight and in less than an hour I was taxiing out to a long, straight stretch of the Chena. For a visual guide to let me know I could safely taxi under the Chena bridge, I used a plank bulkhead built into the bend. When five planks were showing above water, it was a cinch to zip under the bridge to reach the takeoff point. There, after swinging around, I'd have about two thousand feet of water for takeoff.

I aimed the Fairchild at the bridge and poured on the coals for my usual under-the-bridge takeoff that never failed to thrill my passengers.

On the step, the point at which the plane was poised for takeoff, I throttled back a bit to remain on the surface while we zoomed under the bridge supports and girders with a full clearance of just about two feet. Then I gave the Fairchild full right aileron and a little right rudder with full throttle, to pop us out from under the bridge like a cork out of a champagne bottle. I tilted the left wing sharply over the river to yank the left float out of the water. Still linked to the surface with the right float, I could tell by the sound of the engine precisely when I could break free. After we broke loose, I leveled the plane gradually, regaining climb power.

Gaffney and the doctor, seated right behind me, shook their heads at what must have seemed a spectacular takeoff. My under-the-bridge departures usually drew a small crowd of spectators and there were many of them that day.

28

We followed the Alaska Railroad out of Fairbanks past the hilltop university buildings and Ester Creek, where the world's largest gold dredge was clanking away, each of its buckets scooping up about five cubic yards of pay dirt.

After tracing the railroad for about forty miles to where it veered southward, I headed across a couple of ridges where shimmering Minto Lake could be glimpsed just ahead.

I reduced the throttle and pushed the nose forward to power glide to the lake. The engine sound sent clouds of ducks and geese into the sky from the lake.

"Good Lord," Gaffney exclaimed, "there just can't be that many birds over one place at one time!"

As we taxied toward our campsite on the lake, the birds began settling back.

We set up camp near the tied-down ship, blew up air mattresses and got guns and ammunition ready for the next morning's hunt. Volunteer cook Ed Clausen soon had a savory hunter's stew bubbling on the camp stove.

As darkness settled, we snuggled into our sleeping bags, impatient for the dawn to come. Just before dozing off, I heard a low whine from the Labrador stretched out beside his master, whose sleeping bag was next to mine. The dog's tail was quivering and his whole body seemed to be trembling, undoubtedly eager to get down to retrieving. Meanwhile, the pooch was doing everything it could to weld itself more closely to the doctor.

"Mutt sure likes you, Doc," I remarked.

"Yeah," he said drowsily, "besides being crazy about retrieving, he's absolutely bonkers about sharing my bed. The only time my wife lets him sleep with me is on trips like this, so he makes the most of it."

"Maybe he's Cleopatra reincarnated," I suggested, drawing a chuckle from the doctor.

As the doctor began snoring, the dog nuzzled closer, its dark snout fitting smoothly into the curve of the doctor's neck.

By 5 A.M., Ed had bacon and eggs crackling on a large griddle and toast turning gold in another pan. While we ate we could hear a periodic swishing sound — hundreds of birds, early risers, sweeping overhead.

After breakfast, we lined up along the lakeshore about twenty feet apart, kneeling on air cushions positioned in the deep, dewy grass.

"Let's not get too excited," I cautioned, "otherwise we'll be shooting each other. Shoot only at the closest birds."

A couple of large geese swept by overhead. I shot and they tumbled practically into my lap. Within the first hour, I bagged my limit of twenty-four with my 12-gauge German army rifle. After an hour's shooting, the barrel got so hot I had to double up one of my canvas gloves to hang onto it.

"To heck with this grass shooting," Gaffney announced. "I'm going out on the point and get me some fast ones as they come in." He headed for a long sandspit jutting into the lake.

"I'll join you," Carter said.

As they strolled out together, the doctor's dog seemed to be going berserk with pleasure, performing a strange canine dance on his hind legs and yelping with excitement.

Ed and I remained near camp, selectively knocking down big mallards. Once, after the doctor and the dog returned to the camp area, I lost one of the birds behind a tiny island and asked him to get his dog to retrieve it for me.

"Sure you got 'im?" the doctor asked. "Don't want my dog going out on a wild goose chase."

"Positive," I said.

The doctor crouched beside the quivering animal, pressing his head close to the dog's as if deep in some conspiracy. Then, while the retriever remained frozen at attention, the doctor kept whispering to it. When he felt he had his message across, the doctor rose, extended his right hand, index finger pointing to the island. "Fetch 'im!" he shouted.

All but airborne, the dog dashed toward the lake and plunged in with a splash. He began swimming arrow-straight toward the island, joyfully swiveling his dark head from side to side until he picked up duck scent. In moments he located the bird and triumphantly carried it back to his master.

From the start that wonderful dog captivated all of us, beguiling us with his spirit, devotion and undogly know-how. He was right there to retrieve every duck his master knocked down, invariably seeming to know which were the doctor's and totally ignoring ours.

It didn't seem to matter how often we shot — ducks and geese kept swooping past. By four that afternoon, Gaffney had used up his ammunition. Tired but obviously happy, he wandered over and shook my hand. "Never had such hunting, Herm," he said. "I'm sure you'll be happy to know I'm not going to kick your teeth in."

"Thanks a lot," I said. "I guess I should tell you I was planning to get the first kick in." Gaffney, I decided, wasn't such a bad guy after all.

On the return trip, I put the doctor and Gaffney in the two seats just behind me. The dog, obviously reluctant to leave retriever heaven, wedged himself tightly against the doctor's feet, constantly swiveling his head and whining piteously. Ed rode alone, just behind Gaffney.

I loaded the ducks and geese around the passengers and they were soon shoulder-deep in feathers with the dog's swiveling head barely protruding from the bright plumage.

Before starting the engine, I undid the prop bolts with a wrench, washing out two percent in each blade to supply about twenty-one hundred RPMs for takeoff, thus providing optimum hold for the Stinson's nine-foot prop.

Taxiing out, I heard Gaffney say: "You'll never get this damn thing off. Lake's too small."

"Want to bet?" I replied.

I poured on full power and began circling the tiny lake as the floats created ever larger waves on each orbit. Though the newly choppy water brought us up on the step, the stretch of water available ahead was still far too limited for takeoff.

Applying full aileron, I lifted the right wing and right float as the left wingtip skimmed the water. In that configuration, I continued circling the lake, one float in and one float out, gradually picking up speed. Then, a quick jerk on the stick whipped the other float out of the water. We were aloft, picking up speed and power. I saw Gaffney shake his head in disbelief.

"I've seen it all now!" he said.

Gaffney and I became and remain good friends. During World War II he became a brigadier general and commanded Edmonton's Northwest Staging Route, the military's nerve center for getting supplies and planes to the Russian front.

With the onset of war, Dr. Carter entered the Army as a full colonel in command of Fairbanks-area troops. Clausen continued as general manager of the Northern Commercial Company.

The dog? I was so fond of that magnificent animal I was always afraid to ask Carter what became of him.

6

SWINGING BUREAUCRATS

THE MADCAP GEORGE DALE and the sparkling Dr. Evelyn Butler of the Bureau of Indian Affairs in Juneau were a George Burns-Gracie Allen husband-and-wife team. He was clever and mischievous and she was a willing foil for his gags and pranks.

When the government hired me to fly them to Native villages and schools in the Interior and Arctic, I expected to see a pair of stuffed shirts instead of a devil-may-care couple.

Long before such things were accepted, Mrs. Dale used her maiden name professionally.

Dale quickly showed his colors. At Holikachuk on the Innoko River, Dale was having a cup of coffee with the Native school's Juneau-hired teacher, a prim lady in her early thirties.

"Understand you've got a boyfriend," he remarked devilishly.

The poor lady flushed crimson and snapped indignantly: "I most certainly do not have a boyfriend, here or anywhere else. Where did you get such rubbish?"

"Oh, I'm terribly sorry," Dale said, fleeing to safer ground. "It must have been someone else I heard about. Now, about next year's curriculum . . ."

When the teacher left the room for a moment, Dale nudged me and pointed to a framed document on the wall. It proclaimed that the teacher had been examined by the undersigned physician, who certified that as of that date she was a virgin.

The community meeting at Holikachuk was a disaster. Only

six persons attended. Dale was crushed and brooded about it as we flew toward our next stop, Kaltag.

"Herm, I just got a marvelous idea," he announced suddenly.

"Yeah, what is it?"

"Well, we've already demonstrated we can't attract the Natives. Now we need your help."

"Me?"

"You, Herm. For centuries, the Natives have been fascinated by shamans, medicine men — and magic. You're hereby appointed our medicine man."

"Get off it, George. I'm not one of your innocent school-teachers."

"No, I'm dead serious, Herm," he insisted. "I've heard you're pretty good at magic. If you'll put on a show for us it might attract the crowd we need for our pitch."

It was true that for years I had been an amateur magician. And I just happened to have a few of my magic props with me.

"I don't know, George," I said. "I've never been in front of an audience."

"You'll do great," he assured me. "You'll be doing a good turn for the Natives, for the government and, of course, for your business."

"Okay," I said reluctantly, "but if I fall on my face it will be the last time I try to pull your chestnuts out of the fire."

"Great!" he said jubilantly.

At Kaltag, he spread word that a "medicine man" would appear on that night's program. The school auditorium was so packed, some kids had to sit in the aisles.

The Dales got their official pitch in early. Then, after brief-ing the villagers on several programs, Dale introduced me as "a man who brings powerful medicine. Meet Herm Lerdahl, our pilot."

The applause gave me a bad case of stage fright. After an awkward, nervous start, I gradually warmed to the enthusiastic audi-ence and before long was actually enjoying it. I did several sleight-of-hand tricks, made a pack of cards, a handkerchief and a silver dollar disappear, and worked my way up to my best trick, the Magic Knife.

A hush fell as I brandished the glistening fake knife. "Anyone who can't stand the sight of blood can turn their eyes away while I run this knife clean through my hand," I announced. Though a couple of older people turned their heads, none of the kids did. If some idiot was going to de-hand himself, they weren't going to miss any part of it. Swiftly I moved the fake knife over my left wrist after surreptitiously removing the close-fitting half-moon of rubber in the center of the blade. "Aieee . . . !" I heard a little girl scream as the "knife" descended on my wrist and I released a couple drops of red-colored water. Convinced at last that I was committing self-mayhem, a couple of the kids clamped their fingers over their eyes.

"Tell me when it falls, Dad," I heard one little boy up front say.

I quickly removed the phony knife from my wrist and restored the close-fitting cut-out. Then, swishing the restored "knife" overhead, I ran out into the audience to demonstrate that my wrist was okay.

"Great!" Dale said, rushing up as the applause continued.

"Wait till you get my bill," I said.

My "medicine man" act became a regular feature of our village visits. I especially enjoyed entertaining the kids.

On one classroom visit, I chatted briefly with a blonde, blue-eyed teacher after class was dismissed and noticed that a little Native lad had lagged behind and was watching us intently.

As I was leaving with the Dales, the kid sidled up and clutched my sleeve.

"Mister," he said, "we love teacher. You not gonna marry her and take her away?"

"No, son, I'm already married. Maybe, when you grow up, you'll marry her."

"No," he said, grinning, "I love teacher but never marry her. She don't skin muskrats, make mukluks, tan moosehide."

From Kaltag we flew to Koyukuk and were guests at Dominick and Ella Vernetti's roadhouse, which catered to pilots and their passengers and to those who plied the river. Mrs. Vernetti's spaghetti and a bottle of Dominick's vintage wine converted our evening meal into a Neapolitan banquet. On the Vernetti's living room table was a large tablecloth brightly embroidered with multi-colored facsimiles of the signatures of bush pilots who had visited them over the years.

A three-day storm grounded us in Koyukuk, so with nothing else to do I went down to the river to chat with the mushers.

"How many dogs can you hitch to one team?" I was foolish enough to ask. The Natives traded amused glances. One of them, winking at his cohorts, declared: "We'll show you!"

Their eyes glinting with mischief, the mushers hitched several teams in tandem to one of the sleds and invited me to take over. They quickly stepped aside and yelled "Mush!" as I clung to the handlebars. I found myself being swept up the river ice far faster than I had bargained for, going somewhere I had absolutely no desire to go while the rascal mushers roared at my cheechako predicament. I was swiftly being taken upriver by forty-one spirited mutts who showed no signs of tiring. Desperately yanking and struggling, I managed to get the tandem teams halted. Now, however, they anchored themselves solidly to the ice, ignoring all my efforts to budge them. Somehow I got them all pointed back toward Koyukuk. But as soon as I dropped the lead dog's collar, forty-one dogs galvanized into dynamic action and sped off toward the village. It was all I could do to grab the sled as it whizzed by.

Alarmed, I wondered what would happen when they got back to their masters. Would there be a gnashing cartwheel of battling dogs? No, they obediently moved to where the mushers were waiting and submitted to the unhitching and rehitching without a whimper.

"Mister," one of the mushers told me, "you're darn lucky them dogs didn't begin fighting. They like to fight and once they start, nobody can stop 'em."

"As you can see, I'm no musher," I said.

The veteran musher grinned. "If you was, you'd never let yourself be dragged up the river by forty-one dogs."

Dense snow was falling as we landed at Galena on the Yukon. Galena had no visitor accommodations, and when the storm continued the village priest offered to let us bunk in a small room in back of his church.

For two miserable days we were marooned in that cramped, icy enclosure heated only by a tiny oil-drum stove. The first night was awful. With just a thin board between our backs and the permafrost, we began being miserable as soon as the fire sputtered out. We positioned our sleeping bags close to one another to capture any warmth that might offer. The night seemed endless and the first gray smudges of dawn streaking through the frosty window were a godsend. We were glad to get out of there the next morning.

At Wiseman, north of the Arctic Circle, we stayed at Martin Slisco's roadhouse. Slisco, a rather straight-laced guy, studied the Dales closely as they introduced themselves as "Dr. Evelyn Butler" and "George Dale."

"Dr. Butler, I have this nice room for you down the hall," Slisco began. "And Mr. Dale, I'm putting you at the other side of the building in a very nice —"

"Hold on there," the waggish Dale interrupted. "Evelyn's sleeping with me tonight."

"But you're not —" Slisco stammered.

"No problem," Dale declared, capturing his wife of many years in a tight embrace. "When Evelyn and I travel together we sleep together."

The next day, while the Dales visited the school, Slisco joined me over a cup of coffee.

"Are those two married?" he asked.

Slisco frowned when I changed the subject. He seemed uncomfortable the entire two days we were there. For his benefit, the Dales clung together like honeymooners.

That trip was pure enjoyment. I never had better passengers.

7

BREAKING TRAIL

I WASN'T AT ALL PREPARED for the welcome I got at Arctic Village on one of my summertime mail trips.

After I landed my Fairchild 71 on floats on the small lake alongside the village, the Native minister greeted me with a smile and a warm handshake.

"Welcome, Herm," he said. "All my people are here to shake your hand." As he led me down a line of villagers, each smiled and shook my hand.

"I really appreciate all this," I told the chief. "Is it something special?"

He grinned, clasping my hand in both of his. "Lerdahl," he said, "you are a true friend. We love you like a brother. You never bring whiskey to our village. Other pilots —"

I recalled Noel Wien warning me: "Never fly booze to the Natives." I'd followed his advice knowing that, sadly, most Natives can't handle the stuff.

No white person lived at Arctic Village. On Sundays the minister became the Episcopal pastor to his flock of sixty-five. Their rustic log cabin church out on the tundra was beautiful in its rough-hewn simplicity. The altar cloth, painstakingly fashioned by Native women, was a dazzling example of Native beadwork.

The opportunity to reciprocate, in some small way, for the villagers' outpouring of friendship and goodwill came during one of my ham radio contacts with Ray Randall, the U.S. marshal at Fort Yukon.

"Herm, we got word a Native woman in Arctic Village is due to have her baby soon and needs to be flown to the hospital here," Randall told me. "Can you do it?"

"Glad to, Ray," I said. "I'll fly up just as soon as this lousy weather clears."

The Arctic Village weather remained frustratingly sour for nine days, then cleared. On the tenth day, flying the Fairchild on skis, I touched down on the snow-blanketed clearing alongside the row of cabins at Arctic Village. In moments, the pregnant woman was scooting out of her cabin, carrying a large satchel. She was followed by two little girls, about six, obviously twins.

"I knew you'd get here," the mother exclaimed happily.

With their sparkling dark eyes and rosy cheeks, her twin daughters were as cute as a magazine picture. The mother had sewn them bright pink snowsuits with muskrat hoods. They didn't need mittens — she had sewn the sleeves snugly across the ends.

After they were aboard, the ship wouldn't budge. The sixty below cold had glued the skis to the ground. To break free I would have to get everybody off, and then taxi back and forth in the same tracks several times.

I searched my mind for a way to explain to the mother that she and her children had to get off temporarily.

"Please," I said, "You'll have to get off for a few minutes." She looked terribly anxious. "Hospital, please," she pleaded, clutching my sleeve. "Baby coming. Please — hospital."

Suddenly the words "break trail" popped into my mind.

"Yes, hospital," I said. "But first, I have to break trail."

A lovely smile transformed the woman's face. "Yes, I know," she said eagerly. "Break trail."

She seized the twins and tossed them into a snowbank alongside the plane. The tots rolled across the soft surface like furry dolls, then got to their feet and whisked the powdery snow off their faces. I got out and carefully helped the mother down.

After "breaking trail," I stopped and helped the mother and her kids back aboard. Within an hour we were touching down on the frozen river in front of Fort Yukon.

While Simon, the Native dog-musher, took my passengers to the village, I began bedding the plane down for the Arctic night. In less than a half hour Simon was back with his team to get me and the oil to the roadhouse.

"Lady," he called excitedly, "lady — she have twins!"

"Yeah, I know, Simon. I just brought 'em in."

"No, no, Herm, you don't understand. Lady have twins. Two more twins."

I was astounded. "I didn't get here too soon, did I, Simon?"

"You sure didn't."

I shudder to think of what might have happened if we'd started out from Arctic Village a half hour later.

■ ■ ■

Twenty-five years later, as I was driving through Whitehorse on my way to Fairbanks, I stopped at the Log Cabin Tourist Information Center to get a look at the displays of beadwork, mukluks and trinkets from Arctic Village and Old Crow. The small Native woman in charge of the displays kept staring at me, so I walked over, figuring she might be someone I had met.

"A long time ago," I told her, "I flew mail and passengers to Old Crow, Fort Yukon and Arctic Village. Would you happen to know a lady in Arctic Village with two sets of twins?"

She laughed. "My mother," she said. "You got her to the hospital in the nick of time."

"So you were one of those cute little girls in fur suits your mother tossed off the plane?"

"Yes, that was me and my sister."

"You remember me, though you were only six then?"

"Our family will never forget Herm Lerdahl," she said.

8

KUSKOKWIM CROSSROADS

IN OCTOBER OF 1935, McGrath residents chipped in to hire a Fairbanks attorney to defend one of their favorite citizens, "Hi-Power" Johnson. Hi-Power, who did odd jobs around McGrath, got his nickname when he kept boasting what a fine gun his new .22 rifle was, particularly its "high power" feature. The game warden nabbed him for illegally killing moose and distributing the meat to McGrath families for ten dollars a carcass. The citizens arranged for me to fly Hi-Power's attorney, Julian Hurley, in to defend his client.

My navigation on the flight consisted of a pencil line drawn on an old Alaska Road Commission map. Approaching McGrath, I was surprised to see a large pond of unknown depth occupying most of the runway. Coming in, I detoured around the big pond following the half-moon-shaped tracks left by other planes.

McGrath, a busy aviation crossroads, was a mess. Acres of empty five-gallon cans and splintered wooden gas crates littered the Kuskokwim riverfront. Each year, spring floods swept the debris away, and each year pilots restored the clutter.

Bush pilots stayed at a roadhouse-restaurant owned by Dave Clough, who charged a buck a bunk and a buck a meal. At Clough's, you could order anything you wanted, but what you got was either ham, moose or caribou with bread, potatoes and coffee.

Clough's bunkhouse where Hurley and I spent the night was an unpainted, rough-lumber barracks with narrow, double-deck bunks ranged along both walls and a line of single bunks crowding the

43

center section. The sawdust-floor bunkhouse was crowded with about twenty-five men, most of them pilots. I selected an empty bunk in the corner, stripped to my long johns, hung my clothes on wall hooks and crawled into my sleeping bag.

I've been told I'm a pretty fair snorer, but that night I had lots of competition. I heard sawing of logs, hitting of knots, wheezes, snorts, whistles and groans. I heard sleep-talk about a Seattle hooker, sleep-cussing at an Anchorage bartender, and a spine-tingling scream that might have been somebody going over Niagara Falls in a barrel. Finally, I drifted off to add my own contribution to the racket.

The next morning I met Steve Mills, a founder of the old Star Airlines, who had flown in from the Kuskokwim goldfields with Dave Strandberg, a prominent miner.

"In case you're wondering," said Strandberg, pointing to a large leather pouch he had casually leaned against a wheel of Mills' Bellanca, "there's forty-five grand in nuggets in that pouch — one cleanup." In the depths of the Depression, that was fabulous wealth.

"Aren't you worried someone might steal your nuggets?" I asked.

"Naw," said Strandberg, "a crook would be stupid stealing raw gold. Each nugget has its own mark, like a fingerprint. The San Francisco mint can tell right away what Alaska creek the nugget came from and who it belongs to."

Bush pilots who congregated at McGrath were a tough, scrappy, fiercely competitive bunch. Each seemed to have staked out his own jealously guarded flying territory. Gordon MacKenzie, a tall, handsome former World War I Royal Air Force pilot, was one of these. A former barnstormer in Washington state, MacKenzie flew at one time or another for just about all the Anchorage-based outfits, including McGee, Star, Woodley, Mirow and Alaska.

I was startled at the condition of MacKenzie's Fairchild 51, just in from Rainy Pass. Ragged strips of fabric had ripped loose from the top and sides of the fuselage, starting at the windshield and running all the way back to the tail. It looked like a peeled banana.

"What on earth happened?" I asked.

MacKenzie studied me coldly. "You must be new," he said.

"Yeah, first trip to McGrath."

"Well," he advised, "if you ever fly Rainy Pass, count on something like this happening — if you get through at all."

"What did it, the wind?"

"Just fly through Rainy some day, then you won't have to ask."

Without another word, MacKenzie yanked a leather bag out of the baggage compartment and headed toward the roadhouse.

Another pilot I ran into at McGrath was balding, shrewd-eyed Oscar Winchell. Rugged and earthy, Anchorage-based Winchell had been an Arizona cowboy before coming to Alaska.

I was having breakfast when a bearded sourdough beside me asked me what I'd charge to fly him to Takotna. I asked Winchell, who was seated alongside, what he charged and he dodged the question, saying only, "Lerdahl, if you fly to Takotna, you'd better know what a bird knows when it sets on top a telephone pole."

Hi-Power's trial at the schoolhouse began at ten that morning with the commissioner acting as judge. Jury selection took less than fifteen minutes.

The game warden's case against Hi-Power seemed airtight. Hi-Power readily admitted the charges in testimony sounding like a full confession, but Hurley, one of Alaska's finest defense attorneys, wasn't throwing in the towel. He reminded the jury that Hi-Power actually was a compassionate, public-spirited citizen whose only crime was trying to help poor families in McGrath obtain a winter's meat supply at a price they could afford.

It took the jury less than five minutes to reach a "not guilty" verdict. Hi-Power let out a whoop, Hurley beamed and the game warden groaned.

9

UPS AND DOWNS AT WIEN

IN THE FALL OF 1936, my morale was shattered when Ed told me he had to sell the Stinson to raise cash for an auto dealership. To tide me over he offered me a job as mechanic in his garage.

That first week in Ed's garage was sheer misery. I felt like a caged bird.

I was changing a set of pistons on a Dodge one morning when Noel Wien came walking in. "That's no work for a pilot," he said.

I wiped grease from my hands with a rag. "Ed had to sell the Stinson," I said.

"I know, and I hated to hear it."

"You couldn't hate it half as much as I do, Noel."

"I know how you feel. Look, Herm, we can't pay you much at first, but we'd be glad to have you come to work for us — as a mechanic to start with. Later we'll try to give you a chance to do some flying."

"When do I start?" I asked.

"You haven't asked about the pay."

"It really doesn't matter," I said, "but what is it?"

"We can't afford more than a buck an hour until business picks up," he told me, "but I'll see you get as many hours as you want. And you can start tomorrow if it's okay with Ed."

I slammed the hood down on the Dodge, glad I didn't have to work on it anymore. "See you tomorrow, Noel."

■ ■ ■

My first job at Wien was helping mechanics Warren Tillman and "Doc" Bradley overhaul a Stinson SM-8A. We finished it in two days and Noel asked me to join him when he took it up for a test hop.

Noel took the Stinson around once, then turned the controls over to me. "Try a few landings and takeoffs," he said. After several "touch-and-gos," he turned to me. "You handle it very well, Herm," he said. "Drop me off at the hangar and take 'er up again. Then start practicing short field landings."

My world lit up like Roman candles. Though Wien had once told me he'd never hire a pilot with less than two thousand hours because he had too much tied up in equipment to trust an inexperienced pilot, it was clear he was planning to let me do some flying.

After dropping Noel off, I flew the plane on and off the field for another half hour. He was waiting when I taxied up to the hangar.

"Everything okay?" he asked.

"Superb," I said. "You've got some fine mechanics, Noel."

"That's the only kind we hire, Herm," he said. "Right now, I need a pilot. Ever been to Nome?"

"Just once — on skis, last December."

"Well, I've got passengers and freight for Nome, Ruby and Golovin. Feel up to it?"

"Sure I do," I said eagerly. "When?"

"Tomorrow."

■ ■ ■

My first flight as a pilot for Wien was on August 27, 1936. I took off in the Stinson feeling like a kid who's been handed the whole candy store. In Nome, I met veteran Wien pilots Frank Whaley and Johnny Lynn. Whaley began flying out of Nome for Roust Airways before joining Wien. Before that, in the early thirties, he was a prospector and gold miner. Lynn formerly flew out of Nome and Fairbanks for Northern Air Transport.

After that flight, Wien put me on the payroll as a full-time pilot.

I'll never forget my first payday at Wien. Noel handed me a check for $257 at the end of the month. The amount seemed so enormous I thought he'd made a mistake. "That's the most money I've ever earned in a single month in my whole life," I told him.

Startled, he took the check back and tore it into confetti. "I thought we were paying you for only two weeks," he said, slapping his checkbook on the counter and quickly writing out another check, this one for five hundred dollars.

"No pilot's ever going to work for Wien for less than five hundred dollars a month," he said.

The jumbo check left me speechless and overwhelmed. The way things had been going up to then — the sale of the Stinson, being sidetracked to Ed's garage, the hopelessness and uncertainty I'd felt — it all left me unprepared for Noel's kindness and generosity.

My throat constricted and I blinked a couple of times, fighting to keep my emotions in check.

Noting my reaction, Noel added: "You're worth every cent and more, Herm. I can't keep track of everything our bookkeeper does. If you ever fall short of five hundred dollars for a month's work, let me know and we'll make up the difference."

"Thanks, Noel," I said, clutching the check and heading outside, where I could run a hanky over my eyes without being seen.

A year later, Noel named me assistant operations manager. The job didn't pay any more, but that didn't bother me because I felt I was already amply paid. Now, in addition to maintaining contacts with prospective Wien customers, I was responsible for scheduling flights.

Not long afterward, the Wien organization suffered several costly blows. A Wien pilot got careless with a fire pot during an early morning warm-up and a Stinson Reliant went up in flames. A Wien Cessna was totaled while landing at Jack Wade. Wien's old Fokker bit the dust just north of the Arctic Circle while being flown to Wiseman.

The Wiens closed ranks swiftly when the going got tough. Sig Wien completed work on his commercial license and drummed up a lot of new business flying out of Nome. Fritz Wien propped up the hangar operations and the administrative end. Noel himself pitched in with bush flying. For a long time, he and I were the only Wien pilots flying out of Fairbanks. Wien mechanics worked all kinds of hours at rock-bottom wages to keep the planes flying. Despite all these efforts, the financial situation at Wien didn't turn around. I knew things had hit bottom the day Noel came over as I was loading baggage on the Stinson for a mining camp charter.

"We're on the ropes, Herm," he announced gloomily. "Since

tomorrow's payday, I hoped you might have enough in the bank to tide you over if we have to skip a couple of checks."

Noel's request came as a shock. I knew things were bad but I didn't think they were that bad. "Noel, we've got enough set aside to go for at least three months without a check. Go ahead and hold up my checks for as long as you need to."

For months the company wavered between red ink and black, then things began to improve and I was paid in full. I arranged to sell a surplus Bellanca, getting six hundred dollars more than Noel was asking for the ship, thus beefing up Wien's badly depleted bank account at a critical time. The day after the deal was completed, Noel called me into his office. On his desk was a letter and a check from an Anchorage man named McGee who'd bought the Bellanca.

"Herm," he said, "you've worked damn hard for our organization. You showed your loyalty when we hit bottom by dipping into your savings to give us a hand. Though we can't pay you a commission on the Bellanca sale, I think you're entitled to an interest in our company."

He handed me twelve gilt-edged shares of Wien stock worth about fifty dollars each at that time — December 1938. Wien's generous gift helped lay the foundation for a secure financial future.

10

CHRISTMAS 1936

LIKE LOTS OF ALASKA KIDS, my ten-year-old son, Herm, wanted to become a dog-musher. His two malamute pups, Nikkie and Yukon, got so much attention they were spoiled rotten. They practically tore each other apart competing for our affection. The only way we could curb them was to keep them strictly separated. Ed and Bea kept Nikkie and my wife and I kept Yukon.

For Christmas 1936 I decided to get Herm a dogsled Nikkie and Yukon could pull. For thirty-five dollars, a skilled Native at Alatna offered to build a sled for me the way his ancestors built them.

The white-pine and birch sled began taking shape in November. On my trips to Alatna, I enjoyed watching the Native at work on the sled. On one of my trips I saw him steep the runners in boiling water and shape them into graceful curves. Then he lashed the joints together with rawhide caribou sinews. Two days before Christmas, the sled was ready. All I had to do was fly it to Fairbanks.

There was much chuckling and shaking of heads among Alatna's villagers when I began lashing the dogsled to the wing struts of the Stinson. I'd never attempted such a Rube Goldberg thing before and realized that if I crashed I'd have plenty of witnesses to my foolishness.

The entire village turned out in bitter cold to watch me take off. I lifted the plane gingerly off the frozen river. I was determined to drop the lopsided craft back onto the ice if it began pulling too hard to the right. I applied left rudder to maintain directional stability, and was relieved to find I hadn't loused up the aerodynamics.

Somebody at the airport spotted my sled-carrying Stinson as I was approaching, and mechanics converged on the plane as soon as I stopped. They had lots of questions: how did it fly? Any trouble taking off? Much vibration? Control problems? I assured them it was a piece of cake.

On Christmas morning, little Herm was overjoyed when he ripped the bright wrappings off his huge present. He had to get it broken in right away. So, with my brother's help we got the dogs together for the trial run, after borrowing some dog harnesses from our neighbor.

Nikkie and Yukon yipped and cavorted outrageously as we hitched them to the sled. They seemed so dangerously enthusiastic about their first stint at sled-pulling, I insisted on breaking them in myself.

We tied the sled to a post with a line and slipknot, then snapped a twenty-inch line between the dogs' collars. They were so eager to go and so uncontrollable, I had a fight on my hands to keep the lines from tangling.

I scooted to the back of the sled, snatched the lines, tripped the slipknot, and we were off down the trail.

Everything seemed fine until a tiny cocker spaniel popped up right under the malamutes' noses. Terrified, the little animal generated amazing speed as it scooted all the way to the airport. Futilely I kept riding the brake and jamming the runners. Finally the cocker vanished into some brush, and I was able to get the dogs stopped and headed back.

By the time the Fairbanks Winter Carnival rolled around in March 1937, my musher son was trail-tough, having taken his dogs out several times a week. All Herm could talk about was dog-mushing and the coming Winter Carnival race for those in the ten-year age group.

On race day, Ed and Bea, with Nikkie in the back seat, parked directly across the street from where we were waiting with Yukon. When the two dogs spotted each other, wild barking exploded. We knew we had to keep them separated until Herm entered as the sixth team.

As soon as the fifth team got away, Herm scooted swiftly to

the starting line, mounted the sled runners, and waited impatiently for Ed and me to hitch up the dogs. Somehow we got them attached to the sled just before the starting whistle.

Tense with excitement, Herm waved to us as his team whizzed down the street between solid lines of onlookers. He reached the halfway point in far better time than all the other entrants. We caught Herm's excitement and cheered as he streaked to victory in the one-mile race. And we shared Herm's delight as a judge handed him the first prize in his category — three crisp one-dollar bills.

Many times after that I made a point of expressing my gratitude to the Alatna craftsman whose sled-making skill, inherited from former generations, brought real joy to a kid's heart on Christmas 1936.

11

THE STORM

I REMEMBER when I was a farm boy in Minnesota, standing in a grove of trees watching in fear as three tornadoes advanced toward our farm, then abruptly veered away.

During another Cyrus, Minnesota, storm, my mother and dad, my three brothers, two sisters and I had to seek refuge in our basement as the storm raged outside. We clustered together in silence as gust after wild gust battered the house amid flashes of purple lightning and volleys of heavy thunder.

In that storm, neighbors lost barns and outbuildings, fences were ripped out and homes were destroyed. Our house made it through undamaged.

The 1936 Nome storm was, in many ways, just as bad or worse.

The night of the storm I remember walking along the icy boardwalk past the Nome cafe, clinging to window ledges to brace against heavy gusts. That night Jack Stewart had invited four of us to a small-stakes pinochle game at the Pan Am radio shack, which was also Jack's residence. When I got there, the three other players — John Binek, Walter Cavey and Hans Arp — were already there. Red, white and blue poker chips and worn pinochle decks were already on one table, and a side table held a variety of booze and plates of crackers and smoked salmon.

Shelves and counters in the large cabin held Pan Am communications gear, enabling Jack to remain in constant contact with Pan Am flights. There would be no communicating tonight — nobody was flying.

Absorbed in the game, we paid little attention to the occasional wind blasts that shuddered the unpainted, shacklike dwelling. Then, around ten: POW. . . POW. . . POW.

Three powerful sledgehammer blows shook and rattled the building to its foundations. New blasts sent the overhead electric light bulb swaying like a pendulum. Then we heard a strange sound — a high-pitched whistle that grated like wrong-way chalk on a blackboard.

Binek leaped to his feet and shouted, "Sounds like a friggin' banshee."

"Naw," Jack explained, "it's just the keyhole. My keyhole always whistles in a storm. Scared the hell out of me, too, the first time I heard it."

Our interest in pinochle dwindled as the fury of the storm increased. We seemed to be listening with primitive ears to the turmoil outside.

Jack shaded his eyes and squinted at the wind gauge just outside the window. "Holy smokes!" he yelled. "Gusts up to seventy-five miles an hour!"

A moment later we heard an odd, thundering drumbeat on the roof like a string of freight cars rattling over a shaky trestle. Then a metallic, ripping sound and a muffled thud as though something hollow was rolling along the deserted street.

"Betcha somebody's roof just ripped off," Jack speculated. I wondered, would *this* roof hold? How much punishment can a flimsy gold rush structure take? Can a storm of this magnitude destroy the integrity of these thin walls?

I went to the front door and tried to yank it open to get a look at the street outside.

"Won't budge an inch," I said.

"The door opens outward," Jack explained. "Outside, it's packed solid with snow."

I saw Jack squinting through the window at the anemometer outside. "Good God!" he said. "It busted off at 115 miles an hour!"

A dazzling incandescent flash of blue light lit up everything outside for an instant, then the room was plunged into pitch darkness.

"That does it," Arp said, slapping his cards down. "I don't know about you guys, but I'm calling it a night."

"Me, too," said Cavey as the flickering light came back on.

"Yeah, time to quit," Jack agreed. "I'd advise all of you to stay here tonight. So much heavy stuff flying around out there, something could hit you in the head." Nobody insisted on leaving.

Jack passed out sleeping bags and blankets and we strung ourselves out across the floor. I ended up sprawled under the table. Jack switched off the light and somehow, despite the racket outside, we were able to doze.

By nine the next morning the storm eased, though powerful blasts still shook the cabin from time to time. We got the door pried open and went out to survey the damage. There was plenty.

Roofs had been ripped off and windows shattered. A wall of one building had been torn off. Water backed up from the mouth of the Snake River had formed a thick ice ridge all along the breakwater. A row of planes tied down on the river was swamped under several feet of storm-delivered salt water. One of the casualties was a Wien Bellanca.

I was lucky. My plane was tied down at the airport with its nose pointed southwest — the direction of the wind. I had cinched it down with heavy lines to the wing struts and anchored it to two cement dead-men buried in the ground.

12

FLYING THE MAIL

FLYING ALASKA'S MAIL in the thirties had its rewards and headaches. There were times I gladly would have given the job back to the mushers we underbid with the encouragement of the post office.

Wien's mail flights included a once-a-month schedule to Tanacross, 180 miles southeast of Fairbanks, and to Tetlin, another 50 miles beyond.

We regularly lost money on the two bits a pound Uncle Sam paid us for airmail delivery. Sometimes passengers gave us problems on mail flights. A Tetlin nurse chewed me out royally — and deservedly — for subjecting her to a grisly ride. And I got crossways with the Episcopal minister in Tanacross for delivering some wine to a sourdough; more about these incidents later.

Arrival of the mail plane was always a time of high excitement in the villages. Letters, packages, newspapers and magazines created a Christmaslike atmosphere. Reading material was precious and it got passed around until it was in tatters.

Where landing was difficult or impossible, I tied long, brightly colored cloth streamers to mail-filled sacks and usually succeeded in providing front-door or even rooftop delivery. I always tried to include a bundle of out-of-date magazines contributed by Fairbanks newsstands in each delivery.

Most bush pilots routinely did shopping, banking and personal errands for bush customers. I made it a point to check all items carefully to be sure everything ordered was aboard. One Fairbanks store neglected to check the order for a villager in the remote Arctic, with unfortunate results. The sourdough needed a generator for his gas lantern. When it was missing from his order, the poor fellow had to read by candlelight for an entire month.

In Tanacross I enjoyed visiting Herschel and Blanche Fricky and Herb and Flo Okerland. Herb went to bat for me in a sticky situation involving a Scandinavian sourdough, a young Native girl and her jealous boyfriend.

The sourdough, Ole Fredrickson, was a good-natured, middle-aged bachelor who had constructed the log cabin where Pan Am radio operators lived and worked. Wine was one of his weaknesses, and since I'd never heard of him causing trouble, I'd bring him in an occasional jug.

Trouble developed when Fredrickson invited a young Native girl to his cabin to share one of the bottles I had brought him. The girl was with him only a few minutes when her husky young Native boyfriend stormed in, armed with a shotgun. Alarmed neighbors appealed to the Episcopal missionary, who hurried to the cabin with them. When the missionary knocked, lights inside suddenly switched off and shades were drawn. After more fruitless knocking and milling around, the group decided to appeal to Okerland.

"Ole's got a young girl in his cabin and her boyfriend's with them," the minister complained. "He's got a jug of wine and it's Herm Lerdahl's fault for bringing it."

Okerland wasn't sympathetic. "Ole's three times seven plus," he reminded them. "If he and his guests are out of line and breaking the law, you'll know what to do. Otherwise, I'd keep my nose out of it."

They dispersed and apparently there were no repercussions.

Among the stories Okerland told was one about fur trader Herman Kessler's arrival in Tanacross in the early spring, from Tetlin. He arrived just behind the spring ice, poling a sixteen-foot boat. Just about everybody in Tanacross thronged the dock to greet the first river transportation. While shaking hands with Flo Okerland, who had gained a couple of pounds during the winter, Kessler declared, under the impression it was a compliment: "How good you look, Flo — you've gotten so nice and fat."

I played a minor role in bringing matrimony to Herschel

Fricky, a handsome redheaded Pan Am radio operator, and his pretty red-haired wife, Blanche.

During one of my ham radio sessions in 1939, a Montana ham operator asked, "What do you do for a living, Herm?"

"I'm a bush pilot."

"Ever fly to Tanacross?"

"All the time."

"Know a guy named Herschel Fricky?"

"Real well. I'm flying the mail to his place first thing tomorrow."

"Tell him his fiancée, Blanche, will be up two weeks from now to get married."

"Glad to. Small world, isn't it?"

Blanche, a stunning girl with a lovely smile, arrived in Fairbanks two weeks later. I arranged to have a load of freight and mail for Tanacross, so Fricky wouldn't have to charter a plane to claim his bride, and also arranged for an Episcopal minister to be present to tie the knot.

As I nonchalantly unloaded mail and freight at Tanacross, Blanche and Herschel remained wrapped in a prolonged embrace. I visited the redheaded couple many times after that. They were a joy to be with, and even many months later appeared to be still enjoying their honeymoon.

Alaska bush pilots were called on from time to time to do some unpleasant things, and transporting bodies was one of these. Though I handled such matters routinely, I was far from callous or uncaring about the sorrow and tragedy each such incident evoked. I felt a sense of grief when, on my last trip to Tanana before Christmas, I was called on to include in the cargo for Fairbanks the body of an eleven-year-old Tetlin girl who had died three weeks earlier in the Tanana hospital. I felt even worse when I learned that the girl's family couldn't afford to charter a plane to bring the body to Tetlin and had asked Wien to fly her home the least expensive way — as freight. This meant, sadly, that the little girl's body had to be stored in the subzero cold of Wien's hangar until our next trip to Tetlin several days later.

When the time came for that flight, Fritz Wien and I were distressed to find there was so much Tetlin cargo that we couldn't figure out where to put the frozen corpse. Finally we wrapped it in army blankets and placed it on top of other freight in the rear of the old six-place Fokker.

When everything was loaded, the only space left for our passenger, Lucille Wright, a nurse at the Tanana hospital, was on top of the frozen body. We rigged up a seat belt and covered the body with a thick cushion for Lucille to sit on, hoping she wouldn't notice.

At Tetlin I couldn't maneuver Lucille away and had to bring out the child's body. Lucille saw instantly what we'd done and dashed up to me, full of indignation. "You made me sit on top of that dead child all the way from Fairbanks," she said, her eyes blazing. "Outrageous!" Then she spun and walked away. Lucille didn't speak to me for years after that incident.

John Hajdukovich, Tetlin's postmaster and trader, was my favorite old-timer. He always gave the Natives a square deal and they gave him plenty of business. Salmon from Native fishwheels were smoked and packed in forty-pound bundles to be exchanged for rice, coffee, tea, lard, flour and other staples at John's trading post. In spring, the Natives brought in bundles of muskrat skins stretched on metal frames to purchase more supplies or get credit. Many of them used beans to keep track of their credit. If, for example, they had two hundred dollars in credit, they placed two hundred beans in the jar.

A bachelor, John lived alone upstairs in his two-story log-cabin store and post office. Tetlin winter temperatures ranged from forty to seventy below and John didn't dare run short of wood, so he had Native workers stack huge piles of it alongside his house.

On my visits I'd listen spellbound to John's reminiscences of his Austrian boyhood, his world travels as a deckhand on a tramp steamer, and what happened to him after he jumped ship in California. Coming to Alaska in search of gold, he settled in the upper Tanana River Valley, fifty miles west of the Canadian border.

"I'd travel by dogteam to the villages, buying furs from the Natives, but too many times other traders with faster dogs were getting there ahead of me and many times I lost out," he related. "I figured I had to get faster dogs and decided to breed one of my malamutes with a wolf. I tied the bitch to a post outside my store. First night — no action. Second night — nothing. Third night — wolf pounced and they danced around, going at it like gangbusters. Got myself a bunch of half-breed pups. Bred two bitches off those half-breeds and ended up with fourteen quarter-bred wolf pups.

"I was proud of 'em at first, them buggers had lots of power and speed. But whenever they scented moose, caribou or rabbits out on the trail, they took off like dingalings.

"Couldn't control the buggers. Jeez, what a mess! Natives around here are still laughing about my wolf-dogs."

■ ■ ■

I don't believe the residents of Old Crow on the Alaska-Yukon border would have minded it one bit if the boundary had been jogged to include them in the U.S. All incoming and outgoing mail went by way of Alaska, and only U.S. stamps were for sale in the Old Crow post office. This village on the Porcupine River, 180 miles northeast of Fort Yukon, consisted of a trading post, a Royal Canadian Mounted Police detachment and a cluster of Native cabins. Only five whites lived in the village: two fur traders named Ed Jackson and Harry Healy, Corporal Walter Bayne of the Mounties and his wife, and a rugged trapper named MacGregor.

After long years of sporadic mail delivery by riverboat and barge in the summer and dogteam in the winter, the arrival of the monthly mail plane brought high excitement to Old Crow. Native mushers converged on the plane from several directions and pitched in excitedly to help unload the mail. They could hardly wait to get their hands on letters from friends and relatives Outside, packages and the ever-delightful Sears catalogs.

One middle-aged Old Crow Native told me excitedly that he'd learned to read by studying the big catalog page by page. "Best schoolbook I ever saw," he said. "There is the picture and there is the name for it."

On that trip in a four-place Cessna, dense fog wiped out the narrow corridor I'd used to get down to the airport, and in a short time the village was socked in. I didn't mind at all — I enjoyed staying overnight with the Baynes.

As a Mountie, Bayne traveled to remote outposts with a seven-dog team and a Native musher and guide. In relating stories about his law enforcement trips, he said: "You've heard that old saying about the Mounties 'always get their man'? That's B.S."

Killing time the next day, I ran into an old Native woman in a muskrat parka. She was only about four feet tall and, as I learned later, 102 years old. Eagerly she shook hands with me, her toothless grin glowing in a wrinkled, weather-beaten face that was like dark parchment. She posed happily for snapshots and though we couldn't communicate, I found her absolutely charming.

Healy invited us over for dinner that night. Bayne warned me that although Harry was a fair cook, he was known to over-imbibe. He served rum and coke as we chatted before dinner, and I observed him swigging regularly from the bottle.

Promptly at five, he announced that dinner was ready. The table held a large bowl of mashed potatoes surrounded by smaller bowls of vegetables. With the air of a gourmet cook he brought the main course from the oven — golden brown grayling, cooked to perfection, and a platter of fluffy sourdough biscuits. My voracious appetite vanished when I cut into the fish. I put down my fork just as the Baynes were doing the same.

The rum had gotten to poor Healy. In the rush of preparing dinner, he had forgotten to remove the grayling's innards.

"Awful sorry," the host said tipsily when he caught on. "But no big problem."

Humming "Waltzing Matilda," he sashayed to the stove where he kept a large cardboard garbage box. He slid the box deftly up to the side of the table and proceeded to slide all the food-filled plates and bowls into the garbage box. "Nothing to it, my friends," he announced cheerily over the clatter. "You'll like the substitution."

Still humming merrily, he opened two large cans of pork and beans, dumped their contents into a large skillet, made more biscuits and reset the table with fresh plates, silverware and bowls.

After our bean and biscuit dinner we chatted for about an hour, and in all that time not a word was said about the "accident."

The next day Bayne gave me the welcome news that he might have three passengers for me. "These three women need to go to the hospital at Dawson," he explained. "A Dawson pilot asked fourteen hundred for the trip, but they couldn't pay that. Can you help?"

I arranged to fly them to Dawson via Fairbanks for three hundred.

The next morning my passengers were aboard and we were ready to go when MacGregor pulled up alongside with a sledload of furs pulled by one dog.

He handed me a note with the name and address of a St. Louis fur company. "Send 'em out in your name, Herm," he said. "When you get the check, cash it and bring me the money on your next trip." He turned over six large bags bulging with marten and mink pelts.

On my next trip to Old Crow, I brought MacGregor more than seven thousand in cash. Nobody saw anything unusual about such transactions.

In Fairbanks, I put the three Native women up at the Nordale. When they told me they were afraid to venture out into "the big city," I brought sandwiches, soup and coffee to their room.

When I came to get them for the Dawson flight the next morning, I noticed that the two big double beds in the room were undisturbed. They had chosen to sleep on the floor in their sleeping bags.

In Dawson, three dog teams were waiting to take the patients to the hospital. I was glad to provide them this needed transportation at a reasonable price.

13

PHANTOM IN THE FOG

TO THIS DAY I'm haunted by that nightmare flight on December 1, 1937, from Nome to Deering with a half-ton of cargo for Bessie Chamberlain, who operated the Deering Trading Post.

I had made several flights to Deering before, and I expected the 135-mile northward hop to be routine. The weather was perfect: calm, thirty-eight degrees below zero, visibility unlimited. There were no obstacles en route — the tallest peak I'd fly over was only 3,760 feet. My main concern was getting in before nightfall, which settled in fast at that time of year.

The Stinson's skis were off the Nome runway at noon, and soon I was crossing the last low range of hills before I reached my destination. I barely glimpsed Deering up ahead when I saw it — a great, formless mass of Chukchi Sea fog closing in on the village from the north. I had been in the air almost an hour and a half, and with darkness beginning to fall, returning to Nome was out of the question.

Now, Deering was buried in fog. For a few moments I clung to the foolish hope that the fog blanket might lift and I'd be able to scoot in, but it seemed to get deeper and thicker.

I was scared and getting more scared by the minute. The fog had spread until it surrounded me. I hovered in uncertainty over a sea of it — boundless and frightening in its endlessness. It began to swirl around the plane and, feeling desperation, I began to climb on full power until I came out on top. Fog now stretched from horizon to horizon. I felt trapped and helpless as I drifted aimlessly on the billows of that deadly white ocean.

I had no options. I was going to have to go down through that chalky whiteness. Though I had all of Kotzebue Sound to land on, only the ice near the shore would be safe. A couple of miles offshore the ice ended, and a deadly black stretch of open water began. Even if, by some fluke, I was able to get down on the ice, how would anyone find me in all that fog? I could be near Deering or halfway to Siberia. I had to start down.

I throttled back and set the stabilizer for a consistent, slow rate of descent. I was going to have to let the plane fly itself.

Sweat glazed my forehead and palms as I watched the altimeter needle begin dipping slowly. Five hundred . . . four hundred . . . three hundred . . . two hundred . . .

As I moved downward in that swirling whirlpool of fog, streaks of ice began staining the windshield.

One hundred . . . Fifty . . .

The moments that passed seemed endless — and now time had run out. I knew I was skimming the surface, because I felt the plane tremble and heard the gear slithering and slapping on irregularities.

I was down! But where? How far from shore? How far from Deering? How close to open water?

I yanked the throttle all the way back, feeling the skis connect with a long series of tiny ice ridges, praying I wouldn't slam into the cliffs along the shore or hurtle out over the barrier between ice and black water.

Strangely — and alarmingly — the plane didn't seem to be slowing down. For endless moments it seemed to be zooming forward at undiminished speed. Was this some kind of hallucination? At last, blessedly, the plane began slowing. Even so, it seemed to take forever to come to a halt.

The feeling of relief that washed over me at getting down in one piece was fleeting. It was bitterly cold and almost dark. Gray draperies of fog drifting around me made everything outside seem indistinct, spooky. I felt hopelessly marooned out there on the ice, entombed in the fog. If it hung on for a week or more, as often happened, I'd had it. So long as the fog clung to the ice, search efforts would be hopeless.

While idling the engine to burn off gas in the carburetor, I opened the door and peered out. On one side was indistinct grayness, shifting fog, the freezing polar night. On the other, just more dark, shifting halls of fog like restless ghosts moving through catacombs. Nothing — almost nothing. In that first swift glance I glimpsed something out there other than ice and fog.

Something, somebody was out there. A dark figure, as motionless as a statue in a graveyard, was standing near the left wingtip, a vertical snag in a river of night and fog.

Crazy! Chills shivered along my spine. It simply wasn't possible for anyone to be out there! Maybe I'm cracking up, I thought numbly. Maybe I'm dead!

I yelled frantically into the night, just to hear my own voice. "Hey! . . . Hey!"

The cry died in my throat as the figure near the plane began moving slowly and silently toward me, as though a darker section of fog had materialized and was drifting in my direction.

The pieces all fell together and the menace vanished instantly when a grinning Eskimo in a sealskin parka came over. I felt like hugging the guy.

"How did you get here?" I asked.

"I live nearby," he said. "Heard you coming in and came out to give you a hand."

"How far to Deering Roadhouse?"

"You're almost there — I'll take you up."

I drained the oil and installed the motor cover, then dogged his steps as we angled to the shore, about a hundred yards away, and then began climbing an incline toward the blurred squares of light from the roadhouse up ahead.

The door flew open even before we got there.

"Who on earth?" exclaimed the motherly-looking woman outlined in the light from the entrance.

"I'm Herm Lerdahl, with Wien," I told her. "Just flew in from Nome."

"You couldn't have!" she insisted. "Nobody could land in that pea soup out there."

"He sure did, Mrs. Chamberlain," the Native said as he set the oil can down in the corridor. "I was there and saw it — fine landing."

I shook the Native's hand warmly as he left. "Thanks for being out there," I said, then moved into the main part of the lodge.

It was comfortably furnished with overstuffed chairs and polar bear rugs.

As I shed my parka, Mrs. Chamberlain yelled to someone in the kitchen. "Put a moose steak on, Jake, and get the extra room ready." She returned with a bottle of Old Grand-Dad and a glass. "Figured you'd need a shot," she said.

"Thanks a lot," I said, "but I don't drink."

She set the bottle jerkily on the table and stared at me in amazement. "Where in the world did the Wiens ever locate a teeto-taling pilot in Alaska, of all places!"

I just grinned.

The next morning, Mrs. Chamberlain hired two Native youngsters to help me unload her cargo. Nothing had been dis-turbed. In those days, anything a pilot left in his plane overnight was always there in the morning.

The fog had vanished and I had smooth flying all the way back to Nome.

14

MOUNTAINTOP FLYING

FLYING INTO MINING CAMPS in the fabulously rich Forty Mile country was always a challenge. The strip at Jack Wade, two hundred miles east of Fairbanks, for example, was just a rough, pock-marked clearing dozed out of a hilltop ridge raked by crosswinds.

Here each week I picked up Jack Wade's "pot of gold" for delivery to the bank, after I weighed it so I could collect the ten-cents-a-pound freight charge.

The metal bucket usually contained at least twenty thousand dollars in nuggets from the dredge. It was left unguarded outside Jack Wade's "terminal building" — a rickety tarpaper shack.

Jack Wade, the busiest of Alaska mining camps at that time, operated around the clock in the summer and employed around thirty miners and laborers.

As soon as the ice began glazing the creeks in the fall, the camp closed and the miners lost no time in getting to the bright lights of Fairbanks, where they could savor the pleasures of the saloons and sporting houses. Left behind at the camp were several husky Scandinavian lumberjacks, whose job was to cut the wood needed to power steam-driven dredges after breakup next spring. Huge woodpiles would begin to sprout on high ground along the creeks.

Each week in winter I'd fly food and supplies to these hardy Vikings and occasionally I'd accept their invitation to remain overnight.

The nightcaps they'd gulp down before retiring astounded me. They'd boil two heaping cups of coffee for half an hour to produce a syrupy sludge, which they combined with a half cup of Kentucky bourbon. Without exception, each would chugalug a cup of this potent mixture at bedtime without blinking, then topple into bed.

A few miles from Jack Wade was the placer-mining village of Chicken, inhabited primarily by Fred and Anne Purdy, their many children, and the Hawn family.

I flew Hawn into Fairbanks one day and the next day met his doctor, a Dr. Dick, on the street. Over coffee, the doctor told me about Hawn's first appointment.

"Feeling mighty poorly," Hawn told the doctor.

"What seems to be the trouble?"

"Well, you see, Doc, I own this little placer claim at Chicken, and got a couple of fellows working for me. I used to pitch right in with 'em, but now it seems like I get tired all the time and can't hack it like I used to. Something must be wrong with me, Doc. Maybe you can give me some pills. . . ."

"How old are the miners working for you?"

"In their twenties."

"And how old are you, Mr. Hawn?"

"Last birthday, eighty-two," he said.

There were many tough miners like Hawn doing backbreaking work on the creeks though they were in their eighties and even nineties. They were always an inspiration to me.

On February 26, 1937, my thirty-first birthday, I flew a load of freight into Chicken in the six-place Fokker. On my way back over the Goodpaster Mountains, I spotted a tractor laboriously pulling a freight-loaded sled from the tiny runway in the valley up the steep, twisting road to a mountaintop mine.

The tablelike area adjacent to the mine entrance caught my eye. I was sure I could simplify the mine's supply problem by landing and taking off from that mountaintop. I could see streamers of snow whipping off the flat-topped ridge as I made my approach. The Fokker's roar as it settled on the narrow perch several hundred feet above the valley floor brought three men scooting out of the mine entrance.

On full power, I blasted up the steeply inclined ledge and swung the plane to a halt alongside a one-room wanigan where, I figured, the miners ate and slept.

Consternation was written on their faces as I climbed down. I was almost positive nobody had ever landed there before.

One of the miners ran up to me and inquired, "What's wrong?"

"Nothing at all," I said. "Just stopped by to bum a cup of coffee."

"Oh, sure, come in," he said, still looking startled.

They kept studying me suspiciously, their looks seeming to say, "Who's this bird? What's he up to?"

As one of the miners handed me a mug of coffee, he said, "Look, you've got to be in some kind of trouble to land up here like this."

"Not at all," I replied. "Just wanted to stop in on you boys on my way back to Fairbanks from Chicken. Figured someone might want to go to town, or maybe your company might have some freight business for Wien."

They suggested I contact the company's mining engineer at the Nordale. After more chitchat, they asked me to mail some letters.

In Fairbanks I called on the engineer for the Goodpaster Development Company. "Wien can save you money by delivering freight right up to the entrance of your mine," I told the engineer in his hotel office.

The young, dark-haired executive stared at me as though he hadn't heard me right. "You can't land on that mountain," he said.

"I just did. Easy approach, easy takeoff. Had coffee with your men at the mine and they gave me some letters to mail. Here's one for you."

"I'll be damned!" he said, and chuckled. "Maybe we can do business after all."

We got a contract to fly in several hundred feet of narrow-gauge track in twenty-foot lengths — more than thirty tons in all. I didn't tell the engineer that each rail was longer than the Fokker itself, nose to tail.

When I outlined the problem to Ernie Hubbard, our top mechanic, he came up with a solution almost instantly. "All we do," he said, "is remove the inspection plate from the ship's tail and the glass panel from the right windshield. We'll guide each rail in through the window and back into the tail compartment, then tie the bundle

73

of rails to the longerons. We'll wrap heavy gunnysacking around the rails where they contact the windshield, as a buffer."

As I hauled each lopsided jumbo load to the top of the 5,000-foot peak, I had a man from the hangar with me to help unload the rails without damaging the windshield frame, scratching the longerons or rupturing the fuselage.

Though the landings went perfectly, I had to be very careful. I had to approach the ridge on less than full power. As the skis touched down, I had to apply maximum power to pull the ship up the steep grade to the mine entrance.

Just about every day in March, I delivered as many as three loads of heavy cargo to the mountaintop without incident. The flights were challenging to me as a pilot, and highly profitable for Wien.

15

TERROR ALOFT

AT FIRST THERE WAS nothing unusual about one of my early mail flights for Wien, calling for scheduled stops at Fort Yukon, Beaver and Stevens Village.

At Fort Yukon, Bishop Bentley, a powerful six-footer, boarded as a Fairbanks passenger. I was glad on general principles to have him beside me in the gull-wing Stinson. Very soon I was going to owe him my life.

Our Beaver stop was so brief I didn't cut the engine. I remained on the ground just long enough to exchange mail sacks with Postmaster Frank Yasuda.

At Stevens Village, I knew instantly something was amiss. Usually Pete Clements, the postmaster and the only white man in the village of about eighty Natives, had a funny story or a bit of news to share. Today, along with the other villagers gathered at the plane, he was grim and silent.

Mushers came down to the plane with two dogsleds, one to haul the incoming mail and on the second sled, tucked in a sleeping bag, was the motionless figure of a dark-haired little girl. The child's eyes were tightly closed and her skin had the pallor of wax.

"She's just thirteen," Clements told me. "Been running a terrible temperature for days. Unless you get her to the hospital soon . . . "

Two Native youths carried the sick child to the plane, and I had them place her across the three empty passenger seats just behind the cockpit. I wrapped her snugly in wool blankets and gently fastened her to the seat with two seat belts. The emaciated child seemed so deathly still I was tempted to feel her pulse. No time.

Swiftly I swung into the cockpit beside the bishop, who kept turning to keep an anxious eye on the child.

Snow had begun falling softly as I took off, praying I'd reach Fairbanks in time.

I was idly listening to the drone of the engine and fussing with the new two-way radio when a sound, so shrill it jangled my eardrums and sent shivers down my spine, filled the cabin. Then the bishop's head snapped back and I watched in shock as a bloody hand reached forward and began slapping his face violently.

"Dear Lord!" he gasped, so stunned at first that he made no effort to ward off the blows. I swung my head around to look behind us. There was blood everywhere. Somehow, the sick child had unsnapped both seat belts and with berserk fury was attacking everything in sight. I saw bloody teeth marks on a hickory mop handle I had in the back. And I saw where her teeth had sunk into the plane's dural window frames. Blood was pouring from the child's mouth, sending an ugly red stain down her pink cotton pajamas. Some of her teeth had been knocked out; others were askew.

"Grab her — she's out of her head," I yelled as the bishop lunged to restrain her. She twisted from him and flung herself at me with wildcat ferocity, her sharp nails clawing my back and raking my neck. Then her right arm coiled around my throat with incredible pressure.

Choking and gasping, I fought to pry the child's arm loose from my windpipe, but she hung on with maniacal fury.

"Get 'er off me, for God's sake," I managed to gasp out. "Get 'er —" The plane swerved and I righted it.

Using all his strength, the bishop forced the girl backward. Then he unsnapped his seat belt and clambered over the back of the seat, wedging himself between the girl and my back.

"Just fly the plane, Herm," he yelled, rivulets of perspiration pouring across the streaks of blood on his cheeks. He kept her in his grip as she hammered at his midsection with powerful elbow blows. Somehow she whirled out of his grasp and again flung herself at my back. I felt her arm closing again around my throat. The bishop clamped both his arms around her, pinioning her in a tight grip and dragging her off me.

"Think I can hold her now," I heard him yell. A few seconds passed, then he gasped in agony. "Oh, dear God," he moaned. "I think she bit my thumb off!"

I turned as he turned ashen with pain. In mute horror I watched the fingers of his white glove slowly turn crimson and begin dripping blood. Though in terrible pain and exhausted by the struggle, the bishop managed to keep a firm grip on the berserk child.

Now I could contact the office. "Bad problem aboard," I radioed. "Berserk passenger — little girl. Got her restrained but we'll need a doctor and an ambulance."

The child's thrashing and screaming continued for the rest of that awful trip. Never was I so glad to see anything as I was to glimpse the Chena River's wide curve. As we came in I could see the ambulance below and a cluster of people awaiting us. The moment I cut the engine and got the door open, Dr. Dick scrambled aboard, wincing at the bloody shambles.

"It's all right now," he said softly to the child, ignoring the wild screaming. Swiftly he administered a shot into the child's bottom. She began collapsing like a rag doll, and in moments lay limp and motionless.

"Now let me help you," the doctor said, turning to Bishop Bentley, who had removed his blood-soaked glove. Ambulance attendants rushed in and gently placed the limp child on a stretcher. As the doctor bandaged his mangled hand, the bishop watched attendants place the child in the ambulance and he bowed his head. I also prayed the child would be okay.

Next morning I got Dr. Dick on the line. "She's going to be fine after a couple of weeks in the hospital and lots of dental work," he said.

"What got into her?" I asked.

"Prolonged fever and high temperature probably induced temporary insanity," he explained.

"But how could a sick little girl be so powerful and ferocious, Doctor? It was all the bishop could do to restrain her, and he's a big, strong man."

"Even a seriously ill child can muster incredible strength under certain medical circumstances," he informed me. "I know you two had a terrible fight on your hands."

"The bishop had the fight. He kept her off me so I could fly the plane. I never needed anyone in my life so much as I needed him then. Without him, I don't know what I would have done."

A chilling thought struck me: Suppose the bishop hadn't been aboard? Suppose I'd been up there alone with that raging child? Could I have restrained her, defended myself and still kept flying the plane? I knew the answer. No. We would have crashed.

I have never ceased being grateful to Bishop Bentley, who unquestionably saved our lives.

16

CAUGHT ON TOP

I NEVER TOLD ANYONE about the mess I got into in an attempt to fly from Nome to Fairbanks on April 4, 1938.

Four other pilots — veterans all — were trying to get to Fairbanks that day, and had taken off well before my 8 A.M. departure.

Though the weather forecast for the 540-mile flight wasn't too promising, I was reassured that the four others — Art Woodley, Don Glass, Frank Whaley and Johnny Moore — were also in the sky trying to get through.

Flying Wien's four-place Cessna and cruising at 160 miles an hour, I estimated I'd reach Fairbanks in well under four hours. I began following the Bering Sea coast, passing over several villages on Norton Sound.

My first hint of trouble came at Koyuk. There the ceiling had descended to less than a thousand feet. I was encouraged to see the hazy disk of the sun breaking through the clouds from time to time, indicating that the cloud-tops weren't far off.

Just out of Koyuk, I pulled back on the control stick and advanced full throttle to get up on top while I could still see the sun occasionally — not too smart a move in retrospect.

After passing four thousand feet I began getting nervous. Now I was caught between layers with no point of reference to fly by, and no instrument training. Only occasionally did I get an all-too-brief glimpse of the sun; then I was in the soup again. If I tried to descend, I'd probably spin in.

Though I know it's almost impossible for a low-time,

noninstrument pilot to fly right-side-up under such circumstances, I was lucky.

What now? I remembered being told: "Let the airplane alone and it'll fly itself." I wasn't ready to turn loose. I kept my right hand firmly on the throttle, my left on the control stick, and prayed the plane would climb straight ahead.

Flying blind, I was flirting with deadly vertigo, disorientation and disaster. I watched the slow-turning compass with mesmerized fascination, feeling a kind of paralysis and helplessness take over.

I continued to climb skyward — six thousand . . . seven thousand . . . eight thousand . . . nine thousand. . . . Still in the clouds, still blind and sunless, still climbing.

I found myself in a tight turn, climbing fast. My airspeed seemed to be holding steady, and I noted gratefully that the little 145-horsepower, five-cylinder Warner engine was purring like a kitten. But when ice began to build up on the wings, my mouth got so dry from tension I couldn't swallow. I felt caught in an endless maze, blocked from my destination at every turn, beginning to feel real despair.

Ten thousand . . . Eleven thousand . . .

No sun. No blue sky.

Climbing...climbing...climbing.

At eleven thousand, five hundred I began gasping for oxygen; a cold sweat bathed my palms and forehead, and I felt giddy, shaky.

Eleven thousand, six hundred . . .

Eleven thousand, eight hundred . . .

God help me! When's it going to end? Where's that blankety-blank sun?

Eleven thousand, nine hundred . . .

Feeling numb, paralyzed. My mind suggested I was spinning . . . spinning . . . spinning, but the plane seemed to belie it.

Then suddenly, at about forty-five degrees, a tiny streak of light broke the sameness around me and punctured the suffocating shroud that enfolded the plane.

In moments I was out of it, breaking through the solid surface that had been cutting me off from life like a kind of swamp water.

I saw bright blue sky. Sunlight burnishing the smothering clouds. Life-giving sun.

I felt unshackled, reprieved, like splashing around in all that sunlight and sky, but there was no use kidding myself — I was still in the clinches. After struggling my way up, how was I going to get down?

I cast about for an escape hatch, dreading the inevitable descent as much as I had dreaded the ascent. The mind in desperation points you to any straw you can still clutch.

Earlier that week, the Civil Aeronautics Authority had begun broadcasting aviation weather each half hour, and I kept my radio tuned to that frequency. I clearly remembered a segment of the last broadcast: "Shishmaref, clear and unlimited." That had to be my answer. I turned to a 330-degree heading toward Shishmaref on the northwest coast of the Seward Peninsula.

I kept the heading for fifty minutes until, through a mile-wide hole in the overcast, I could see a small, brush-edged lake far below. I had found my escape hatch and lost no time in heading down, spiraling to avoid the fringes of the invading soup.

Should I try to land somewhere and spend the day waiting until it cleared? I got my answer on the fourth orbit of the lake. Off to the side, I spotted a couple of gently curving lines on the tundra, the Kougarok Railroad. I felt like singing now that I knew precisely where I was.

I banked to the south and began tracing the tracks from about two hundred feet, traveling as slowly as I could without stalling — I didn't want to lose sight of those beautiful tracks for a second.

Besides, the clouds were right around me again.

What a roller-coaster ride! That railroad kept turning like a snake in torment. Repeatedly I found myself banking until a wingtip was skirting a hillside, then banking just as steeply in the other direction as the clouds dropped down on me with leaden weight, forcing me even lower than it was safe to go.

Eight miles from Nome I broke into clear weather and could see the ramshackle gold rush town clinging to the Bering Sea just ahead to the south.

I felt bad at having had to turn back, convinced that the other four pilots had been able, somehow, to plow their way through.

My spirits soared when I saw all their aircraft parked at the airport.

None of us made it to Fairbanks and I almost didn't make it. But I didn't tell anybody.

17

NIGHTMARE AT 46 BELOW

FOR ME THE NIGHTMARE that haunts every bush pilot began on my way back to Fairbanks from Tanana in a Stinson SR-8, where I'd picked up four hundred pounds of dried dog salmon for one of Wien's Fairbanks customers.

Below was a desolate, forbidding, lake-studded wilderness, trackless and empty as far as the eye could see.

I was cruising at forty-five hundred feet, idly studying the frozen wasteland that stretched from horizon to horizon, when the engine cowling suddenly began vibrating wildly and the engine began running rough as a buzz saw. Piston trouble!

The plane started losing altitude immediately. Like it or not, I was going down. I wondered whether the speed and power I had left might get me as far as Minto Flats, where there were all kinds of places more suitable for a forced landing.

I throttled to half power, tracing a wide arc to the left to pick up a westerly course in the direction of the flats. Though the engine functioned better at half-throttle, I kept losing altitude alarmingly. Now I was less than a thousand feet above the terrain and dropping steadily. There was not much time to pick and choose an ideal ditching spot in those final moments — I had to select just about anything available. I spotted a small, frozen lake edged by stunted trees. In moments I was skimming the tops of small trees near the irregular shoreline.

Billows of powdery snow sweeping past the cockpit and a shivering thud told me the skis were skimming the ice. Producing a wide white swallowtail on both sides, I plowed on toward the center of the lake for more than a hundred yards. Unless it snowed again soon, the deep gash in the snow from the shoreline to the center of the lake might catch the eye of searchers.

I had no illusions about the seriousness of my situation on that bitterly cold day — February 11, 1938. Finding a lost plane in hundreds of square miles of dead-white wilderness terrain, particularly if the weather turned nasty, could become a needle-in-the-haystack endeavor. I might be in for a long, long wait. One thing I knew — I would stay with the plane, to the end if that had to be. There had been cases of pilots trying to hike out through the wilderness with tragic results. I'd never attempt anything like that.

Though I had no radio to get word out, I knew the search would get under way automatically when I failed to show up.

I slogged through the foot-deep snow, noting strings of animal tracks here and there, and checked under the cowling. What I suspected had happened: a cylinder had torn loose from its base.

I checked the thermometer: forty-six below zero. Then I drained the oil and covered the engine.

I dug out my emergency rations and lighted the fire pot to begin melting snow so I could brew some tea. I found that at forty-six below, a cup of hot tea turns lukewarm by the time it gets to your lips.

Next I tried to whip up some pancakes, but succeeded only in concocting a couple of soggy, tasteless circles of dough. Even so, I gobbled them up. Canned sausages warmed on the fire pot tasted better. It turned out that the fire pot either scorched the food or flickered out altogether. I finally gave up and stowed the rations in the baggage compartment.

To clear a sleeping area inside the plane, I had to remove the four hundred pounds of dried salmon from the cabin. I stacked the bundles of fish outside, knowing the scent would attract wolves and other animals, but there was nothing I could do about it. To scrounge sleeping room in the plane, I arranged seat cushions in an irregular line and wriggled into my eiderdown sleeping bag, prepared to settle down for the long, dark, cold night. I couldn't stretch out and I felt cramped and miserable as I stared glumly into the darkness.

Even after body warmth began to make the sleeping bag more comfortable, sleep eluded me. I dozed only fitfully until around midnight, when I was jolted upright by a shrill, long-drawn-out, mournful cry that tapered into silence, then was joined by others. Wolves! I settled back uneasily in the darkness.

The .22 pistol in an overnight bag near my right hand offered some comfort, but I wondered whether it could hold a wolf pack at bay.

Sporadic howling continued into the early morning hours, then began to subside. The intervals between wolf choruses grew longer. Finally, totally exhausted from weariness and strain, I drifted off.

In the bitter cold of the new dawn, I ventured into the icy grayness to reconnoiter. About one hundred feet from the plane, wolf tracks formed an irregular circle. For some reason they hadn't moved in closer. Would they still keep their distance in the coming night?

Beyond the lake's eastern shoreline stood a thin stand of stunted timber that looked inviting. I could build a fire there, put up a shelter, and maybe be a little more comfortable. But tempting as it was, I realized that the plane offered superior shelter. Besides, I wanted to be close to the plane when a search plane flew over.

The silent hours of that first day dragged by tortuously. I wandered aimlessly around the area, never venturing far from the plane. I scanned the skies, listening, impatient for rescue to come.

Occasionally I'd sit on a five-gallon oil can just under the motor cover. I warmed up another can of sausages, then whipped up some biscuits that didn't taste bad when washed down with a cup of chocolate.

Every waking hour I kept scanning the skies, hoping the sound of an engine would break the silence. I felt intense loneliness, felt cut off and abandoned as though I were a castaway on the moon. My mind kept conjuring up the simple things we take for granted in civilization: a warm bed, a cup of hot coffee, being able to talk to another human being. I felt a vague hopelessness about the approaching night. Depressed and miserable, I crawled back into my sleeping bag when darkness came.

Less than an hour later the wolves began moving in closer to all that dog salmon, howling and circling. In my mind's eye, I could see them advancing, their sharp fangs wide, their fire-opal eyes glowing in the boundless night. What would those devils do next? Would they rush right up to the plane? Try to get in?

As they circled, I felt like the bull's-eye in a target, under siege as I listened to the unearthly guttural howling. I reached over to feel the gun and check to see that the chambers were loaded.

Well after midnight I drifted off into troubled sleep, to be awakened by the gray smudge of dawn light spilling into the plane. I got out and reconnoitered again, my legs and shoulders aching from long hours in a cramped position. I noticed the wolf tracks had moved closer to the plane, but the pile of dog salmon so far had not been disturbed.

Throughout the third day I kept feeling down in the dumps. I tried to force myself to think positively, kept trying to reassure myself that rescue might be only hours away. I was far from successful in fighting off the gloom that had settled on me.

I wondered: were they ever going to find me?

I patrolled around the plane in ragged, aimless circles, knowing that each passing day reduced my chances for survival. As I sat on the oil can waiting, listening and watching, I saw what looked like a plane streaking across the western horizon. My spirits soared until I realized there was no sound and it must have been a bird.

Even though I could start on the dried salmon when the rest of the food was gone, I thought it best to begin rationing myself strictly. I might be able to hold out for several weeks. I tried not to think about the ordeal that lay ahead.

Late in the afternoon of the third day I heard what sounded like an aircraft engine. I whipped off my parka and began circling my plane, waving the parka. The plane drew closer and headed toward the lake, then dipped for a landing. Now I could see it was a yellow gull-wing Stinson.

John Cross of Kotzebue flew a plane like that, I knew, and I figured it was John. The pilot taxied toward my plane as I stashed the fire pot away, rolled up my bedroll and locked the plane. Even before the propeller of the Stinson stopped and the door opened, I was climbing in.

In moments we were off the lake and heading to Fairbanks. I was happy to see that terrible place disappear beneath the wings of John Cross's Stinson.

The next day I flew to the lake with another pilot to replace the busted cylinder. What was left of the dog salmon had been thoroughly shredded and strewn about.

Alaska Album

Herman Lerdahl, wearing a Native-fashioned parka. This photo was taken sometime in 1943 or 1944 while Lerdahl was flying for Northwest Airlines.

Among his many regular stops, Lerdahl delivered mail and cargo to Tanacross, home of the Tanah Indians (his plane here is a Stinson SM-8A). A dog team prepares to haul the load to the tiny village on the Tanana River.

Lerdahl's career with Wien took him to many outlying Native settlements. This photo, from the mid-1930s, shows Lerdahl with a Native. The inscription on his cap reads "Wien Alaska Pilot Fairbanks."

Bishop Bentley, an early-day missionary, is credited by Lerdahl with having saved his life in a harrowing adventure aloft. Behind Bishop Bentley is the Wien Cessna Airmaster.

Malamutes Nikkie and Yukon joyfully race along a Fairbanks trail, guided by ten-year-old musher Herm Lerdahl, Jr. The sled, constructed by an Alatna Native, was the boy's Christmas present in 1936.

The side of Aniakchak volcano became an improvised landing strip for Lerdahl's Howard D.G.A.
Photo courtesy of the National Park Service

George Dale and Evelyn Butler, Bureau of Indian Affairs officials, are shown with Arctic villagers (and behind them the Stinson SM-8A). Lerdahl flew the couple over 4,000 miles to numerous Alaska villages.

A welcoming committee, sometimes 50 strong, turned out whenever the plane arrived with mail and supplies for an outlying village.

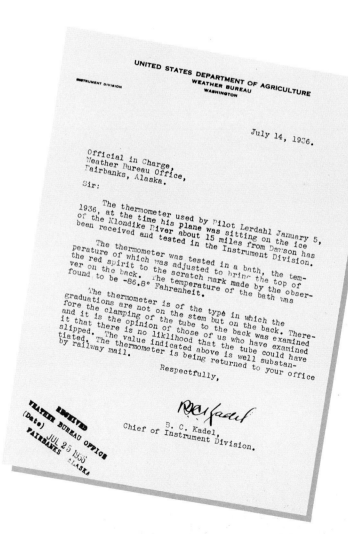

INSTRUMENT DIVISION

UNITED STATES DEPARTMENT OF AGRICULTURE
WEATHER BUREAU
WASHINGTON

July 14, 1936.

Official in Charge,
Weather Bureau Office,
Fairbanks, Alaska.

Sir:

The thermometer used by Pilot Lerdahl January 5, 1936, at the time his plane was sitting on the ice of the Klondike River about 15 miles from Dawson has been received and tested in the Instrument Division.

The thermometer was tested in a bath, the temperature of which was adjusted to bring the top of the red spirit to the scratch mark made by the observer on the back. The temperature of the bath was found to be -86.8° Fahrenheit.

The thermometer is of the type in which the graduations are not on the stem but on the back. Therefore the clamping of the tube to the back was examined and it is the opinion of those of us who have examined it that there is no liklihood that the tube could have slipped. The value indicated above is well substantiated. The thermometer is being returned to your office by railway mail.

Respectfully,

B. C. Kadel,
Chief of Instrument Division.

RECEIVED
WEATHER BUREAU OFFICE
(Date) JUL 25 1936
FAIRBANKS ALASKA

One early morning in Dawson, Lerdahl took off in the Stinson SM-8A when the temperature was colder than 85° below zero. The fact was officially verified by the U.S. Weather Bureau in this letter, one of the pilot's prized mementos.

On June 3, 1942, buildings at Fort Mears in Dutch Harbor were set ablaze by attacks from Japanese Zero fighters based on carriers of the Imperial Northern Force. The sudden attack, at a time when Alaska was skimpily defended, dealt a paralyzing psychological blow to the Territory and underscored the importance of pilots like Lerdahl, who flew men and supplies to defense sites in the Aleutians that were being feverishly bolstered.
Photo courtesy of Alaskan Air Command

Leon B. "Slim" DeLong was Morrison-Knudsen's construction superintendent in Alaska just before and during World War II. DeLong hired Lerdahl as MK's first pilot. Here DeLong is shown as a Lieutenant Colonel in January 1943, after the Army "drafted" him to direct projects for the Corps of Engineers.
Photo courtesy of Alaskan Air Command

This rare historic photo shows some of Alaska's pioneer bush pilots who participated in the whirlwind Nabesna-Northway freight haul project. From left: Merle K. (Mudhole) Smith (Cordova), Rudy Billberg (Fairbanks), John Walatka (Anchorage), Frank Barr (Fairbanks) seated on barrel, Don Emmons (Fairbanks), Jack Scavenius (Anchorage), Frank Cramer (Fairbanks), and Herman Lerdahl (Fairbanks).

This young couple, with their year's supply of provisions, was flown to their wilderness cabin site by Lerdahl. They were typical of the many Alaskans who depended on early-day pilots. The aircraft is a Cessna Airmaster.

Lerdahl was forced down on a wilderness lake in the dead of winter — the only forced landing in his career. His cargo of dried salmon is stacked near the tail section of the plane (a Stinson SR-5). The salmon brought wolves in close before rescue came.

During the war, Herman Lerdahl flew a DC-3 for Northwest Airlines on the route between Anchorage and the Aleutians — a route that offers some of the world's worst weather.

18

TOUGH, AS IN SOURDOUGH

LOOKING UNCERTAIN and embarrassed, the two husky sourdoughs kept eyeing me as I made preparations to take off in the Cessna from Alatna, on the Koyukuk River, to Fairbanks in late December 1938. They stood outside Don Evans's trading post.

I saw one of them push the other toward me with the words, "You tell 'im, Ernie."

The taller of the two approached me reluctantly. "Mr. Lerdahl," he said haltingly, "I'm Ernie Johnson. Dis is my brother, Rudolph. Vee need to go to Fairbanks."

"Got room for both of you," I said. "Hop in."

"But vee got to tell you von ting. Vee . . . broke. In Fairbanks vee get chobs — den vee pay you. Okay?"

Though I got stung a couple of times, I never turned down anybody in such circumstances. Besides, I liked the looks of the Johnson brothers. Though broke, they were still in there fighting.

"Sure," I said. "Get aboard."

The Johnsons told me that they had come to America from Sweden in the 1890s and, after a couple of years in the Northwest, headed for Alaska to seek their fortunes. They took part in several gold rushes but the bonanza they kept hoping would come their way always eluded them. Now they were determined to start out from nothing once again. I had to admire their spirit.

The pair lost no time in scrounging up labor jobs and, after paying me as promised, began squirreling away every spare cent. Meanwhile they lived very frugally in a flophouse near the Chena.

"Vee about ready to go home," Ernie told me plaintively one day in early spring. "Fairbanks not for us. Vee vant to go back to our cabin."

By mid-April they had accumulated about six tons of food, supplies and mining equipment and assured me I'd be able to get into their place, known as Johnson's Landing, with no trouble. I had learned very early that a sourdough's conception of a suitable landing field rarely coincided with mine. A field they described as "real good" could be a gravel bank on the curve of a river, a postage-stamp clearing in a forest or a clear space on a steep hill. The Johnsons, however, insisted there was "a damn good" runway near their cabin and that it was fifteen hundred feet long and a hundred feet wide.

We arrived over the wilderness cabin in extremely remote country, about 260 miles northwest of Fairbanks, on a bright, clear April day. I circled the field a couple of times in the Cessna and dragged it once. Though the snow appeared quite deep, I decided it was feasible.

I made my approach with very little power, setting down gradually and gingerly. Down we settled, down, down, and down some more, the plane's skis and belly plowing through almost six feet of powdery snow. At the end of our landing roll we were literally tunneling through the stuff for several hundred feet.

"Jiminy — vee never tot dis snow vas dat deep," Ernie exclaimed.

I told them we'd better start tamping it down or we wouldn't get out of there until next summer. Unless we did that, and promptly, getting off the field would be impossible.

All of us strapped on snowshoes and began tamping. With every step we took, we had to lift our snowshoes high before setting them down again. It had to be done in that painstaking way.

As the long night wore on, we worked ceaselessly under a bright Arctic moon, advancing up the field at a snail's pace until we had compressed an area long enough for takeoff. That took up more than ten hours of bruising, strength-draining work, and left me so worn out I could hardly walk. The Johnsons, by contrast, seemed to still have plenty of spare energy.

At about 2 A.M., with pale moonlight silvering the tiny "get-away" area, I told them it was adequate and we could knock off. The trek to the Johnson cabin, about a quarter of a mile away, seemed endless. I was so exhausted I could have slumped on the snow and passed out, but I didn't want to let the Johnsons see how done in I was.

We took turns breaking trail. By the time we got to the cabin, I was staggering along like a drunk, listlessly dragging a sleeping bag behind me. The Johnsons still seemed fresh and strong, though they each had about twenty years on me.

When we got to the cabin I was hardly able to shuffle across the room to the bunk, where I collapsed, going out like a light in clothes soggy with perspiration from those long, backbreaking hours of tamping. Having kept active all their lives, the Johnsons were in far better physical condition than I was. Other than running around to hotels and rooming houses to drum up business, I got very little exercise.

What seemed like a light rain falling on my face awoke me. To get a draft, the Johnsons worked a long stick repeatedly up the stovepipe, unclogging a winter's accumulation of snow. As warmth spread through the cabin from the fire they kindled, droplets of moisture from melting frost on the ceiling began to rain down. Rudolph draped an old tarp over my sleeping bag to keep it dry, and let me snore away. About an hour later he brought over a large bowl of warm milk and oatmeal, liberally mixed with honey. I wolfed down the wonderful stuff from a sitting position on the bunk. Never have I tasted anything so delicious, so warming and nourishing. After enjoying a steaming cup of chocolate, I conked out again, snoring up a storm, they told me later.

Rudolph shook me out of a sound sleep around nine the next morning. The weather was clear and soon it was a bright, sunny day, though the temperature remained around thirty-five below.

Ernest was out at the ship with the fire pot, warming up the engine. The plane's oil was heated in a five-gallon can on the stove until it was hot enough. These fellows knew exactly what to do.

After a breakfast of more oatmeal and honey I felt somewhat restored, though my muscles still ached terribly.

Rudolph lugged the hot oil to the plane and I poured it in as Ernest proceeded to break the skis loose from the ice. I threw the prop over by hand and the engine started at once. With Rudolph holding fast to one wing and Ernest the other, I was able to apply enough power to pop the plane out of the depression and onto the newly tamped, solid snow. I was in the air before noon.

I gave the Johnsons a week to enlarge the landing area, then brought in the rest of their cargo in one of our larger ships. I had no trouble getting in on the field — the Johnsons had enlarged it to a length of about a thousand feet and a width of thirty feet.

I spent the night with them and dined on delicious fresh moose steaks, hot biscuits and gravy. This time the Johnsons had enough supplies to last them a year or two. They even had a battery radio so they could listen to the Richfield Reporter. They were eager to pitch in for a fresh start.

In the years since that trip, I have lost track of the Johnsons. They may have died unmourned in their wilderness cabin. I hope not. I hope they are still out there challenging the worst this tough land can hand out. I hope some nuggets and some good living have come their way somewhere along the line, because if anyone deserves it, the Johnsons do. For me, they symbolize the spirit, toughness and determination of Alaska's pioneers. They left an indelible impression.

19

FOKKER ON FIRE

TWO OF MY WORST flying experiences in Alaska involved a kind of dodo bird of an airplane that might have been put together by a committee: the six-place Fokker.

A real Jonah, the Fokker's long, fabric-covered fuselage was topped with a high plywood wing. A remarkably long exhaust extended to just above the cabin door.

In the Fokker's cockpit, the pilot and co-pilot were elevated and isolated from the rest of the plane and able to see very little. It was not designed for maximum pilot visibility. Few Alaskan bush pilots ever had a kind word for this awkward old bird. I never liked it to start with, and liked it even less after two harrowing incidents that still give me a chill when I think of them, one at Fairbanks, the other at Wiseman.

The first near-disaster occurred in Fairbanks while I was taking off in the Fokker on skis with six passengers. The plane caught fire just as we became airborne — and I wasn't aware of it. Just as we got off, raw gas overflowed from the carburetor and seeped onto the hot exhaust pipe, bursting into flame. Flames began licking along the oil-soaked fabric on the bottom and sides of the rear part of the fuselage.

Something inexplicable saved us. Moments after takeoff the right wing tilted abruptly, forcing me to abort the flight and make an emergency landing in a farmer's field even before I knew we were on fire.

When the Fokker came to a halt, I was shocked to see

passengers bursting frantically out of the emergency exit at the left side of the plane and rushing away.

Puzzled, I pulled the lever that snaps the hatch open, stuck my head out, and turned to look over the back of the ship. Only then did I see the tongues of flame and billows of smoke pouring from the rear part of the ship.

Fire! I moved fast. I scooted out on the Fokker's wing until I reached the very tip, and jumped. Just then an emergency vehicle rolled up and men with fire extinguishers promptly put out the blaze. The damage was amazingly light when you consider what could have happened. Though fabric on the bottom and sides of the fuselage was badly charred, there was virtually no damage to the upper section.

Most fortunate of all, there were no injuries, though one of the passengers, a fifty-eight-year-old man, was taken to the hospital in shock. He died that evening — the only passenger casualty I've had during my entire flying career. His death dealt me a shattering mental blow. I tried to console myself with the thought that everyone else came through safely.

Why did the wing dip sharply as though some unseen hand was forcing it down? Pilots, engineers and mechanics I discussed the matter with couldn't give me an explanation, even a theory, and it's a mystery to this day.

The following summer I was flying the same plane to Wiseman when another horrifying incident occurred.

Everything seemed normal as I prepared to land on Wiseman's 550-foot airstrip. Coming in, I could see a cluster of people on one side of the field — just about everyone in the village turned out to greet the mail plane's arrival.

I also saw a lone figure standing about a hundred feet from the end of the runway directly in my landing path. It was the schoolmaster, George Rayburn, who usually stood there when I came in. Ordinarily I'd have no problem in stopping well before I got to George. The Fokker's hydraulic brakes assured firm control, once the heavy-duty tires on the gear touched the runway. I'd get the plane slowed down promptly by locking one wheel and swinging the plane around in its own length at the appropriate time.

Good approach, smooth landing, perfect rollout — then, horror. I started to apply the brakes with the stick all the way back to keep the tail down. A spasm of shock hit me as I realized the pedals were moving downward with no resistance. No brakes! Worse, Rayburn had no way of knowing I couldn't stop and there was no way I could warn him. Horror-stricken, helpless, I watched as the plane advanced relentlessly on the unsuspecting victim. It would be only moments before the propeller began chopping him to bits.

My first thought had been to let the plane proceed to the end of the runway, then groundloop it with a blast of power to the left. I couldn't do that now — Rayburn was standing right at the spot where I planned the maneuver.

I was screaming silently as the distance between Rayburn and the plane narrowed to only a few feet. I don't know how he did it, but with just a second or two to spare, George lurched violently to the side, cheating death by mere inches. As I hurtled by, I got a glimpse of Rayburn's face, distorted in fear. I was every bit as scared, since I was forced to ride it out to the end of the field where a four-foot ditch intersected the flight path.

The plane hit the ditch with a wrenching, splintering sound. I sat paralyzed as the landing gear sheared off. I was in a state of shock, expecting the Fokker's engine to come busting loose to land in my lap. Mercifully, the engine remained in place.

Without knowing exactly how I got there, I found myself standing, dazed and shaken, on top of the wing with the hatch open. Quickly I climbed down to inspect the damage. It consisted of a few bent struts and a couple of sheared fittings on the landing gear. The engine was undamaged.

Rayburn had escaped a horrible death, but the experience must have left a lifelong mark on him. Neither he nor any other resident ever again ventured onto the runway when a plane was coming in.

Though I try not to dwell on that hair-raising incident, I have always kept a warm spot in my heart for the people of Wiseman. I think often of Martin Sliscos and his wife, who ran the roadhouse and trading post, and Joe and Tishu Ulen, who operated the post office. Another Wiseman resident I remember well was a man named English, whose son Bill later became a B-737 captain for Wien and one of the company's largest stockholders.

Among my prized possessions is a slipper-shaped gold nugget presented to me by the Ulens in an appreciation ceremony attended by everyone in town.

20

JOURNEY TO NOWHERE

MAYBE IT WAS BETTER that I didn't know the truth about the two sinister characters who invited me to their room in the Nordale Hotel on June 12, 1940. Not knowing who or what they were kept me innocent and naive about the kind of trouble I might be getting myself into.

Criminals don't necessarily look like criminals, but these guys looked as if they'd just stepped out of the cast of a movie about Al Capone. One of them was pasty-faced and pockmarked and had the cold, predatory eyes of a weasel. The other had a nasty knife scar zigzagging vertically down his right cheek, and the shoulders of bull.

I later found out that they were every bit as dangerous as they looked. Both were fugitives on the FBI's "Most Wanted" list, and if I'd been on my toes, I would have remembered seeing their mugs in the post office. And to add spice to the mystery that might have come right out of a gangster novel, the FBI later informed us that the two men were headed, for some strange reason, for the Soviet Union.

I didn't, of course, have the slightest inkling that these were very bad hombres when I knocked on the door of their room at the Nordale.

"You the man from Wien?" a voice came from within.

"Yes."

Scarface opened the door only a couple of inches and studied me coldly, then opened it all the way. "Come in," he said. "We've got a job for you."

95

A huge map showing the Arctic Coast and portions of Siberia was rolled out on one of the beds. "Here," Scarface told me, jabbing a section of the map with his forefinger. "You're gonna fly us here, to this place on the Marsh Fork of the Canning River."

I couldn't figure out why anyone would want to fly to such a desolate, forbidding spot. What, I wondered, could they possibly be thinking of doing, four hundred miles north of Fairbanks near the Arctic Ocean?

"Rough country," I volunteered. "Deserted. Not a soul around for hundreds of miles."

"That's where we want to go," he snapped. "We don't need your opinion. What's the charge for two passengers and five hundred pounds of cargo?"

"Trip that distance will run you around six hundred dollars."

"Good," said Weasel, his animal eyes glaring at me. "Where do we meet you?"

"Tell the cabbie to take you to the float-plane landing just east of town, near Busby's farm. We'll be flying a Fairchild on floats and I'll be ready to go at nine tomorrow morning."

Though I was feeling active dislike for both these oddballs, I reminded myself that my job was to get as much flying business as I could for Wien. Who my passengers were and why they wanted to go somewhere was really no business of mine.

The next morning when I saw their baggage, I thought it was just as peculiar as they were. They had an odd collection of heavy duffel bags, more guns than any two men could possibly need, and a strange assortment of chrome tubing.

We had no trouble until we got to Fort Yukon. With a full load of fuel and all their odd baggage, there was too much of a load to get off the river in the dead calm air. Three times I tried to jockey the stubborn six-place Fairchild aloft, and each time it insisted on remaining on the surface. After each unsuccessful attempt, I had to taxi back to Fort Yukon to top the tanks again — I didn't dare leave for such a remote spot without a full load of fuel.

Weasel screamed at me. "What the hell's going on? Why ain't we goin' somewhere? This goddamn yo-yo stuff better stop."

I tried to explain the float-flying problem as simply as I could, but I knew I wasn't getting through. "All we need is a little bit of wind," I said. "We need —"

"We need to get goin', goddamit," said Scarface, fixing me with a cobralike stare.

I hadn't expected all this hostility and turmoil, and for two cents I would have flown them right back to Fairbanks, but I thought better of it.

I was glad to see a thunderstorm approaching off to the southwest. When the storm reached Fort Yukon, I figured it would generate enough breeze to roil the water sufficiently for our takeoff. Less than an hour later, sizable ripples began dappling the water. In rougher water, I got off the river without a problem.

From Fort Yukon it was a straight shot to the headwaters of the Canning, after crossing the Brooks Range and the Philip Smith mountains. We skirted the Beaufort Sea watershed near the ocean and soon were above the Marsh Fork. In its higher reaches the river was a series of treacherous cascades and huge boulders, but below, where tributaries joined, it was deeper and wider. After some reconnoitering I spotted a fairly long, straight stretch of fast, deep water and put the plane down in the swift current. I blasted upriver until I spotted a sloping beach on the left side of the snow-fed stream, and shallow water alongside.

After we got the luggage off, Weasel brought out his billfold to pay for the charter. I told him I had misjudged the distance by two hours so would have to add another hundred to the bill. To my surprise, he peeled seven hundred dollars in twenties off a huge roll without protest.

I made the mistake of asking, "Where can I pick you up for the return trip?"

The tough guys traded swift glances, then glared at me.

"You're not picking us up," Weasel snarled, his cold, beady eyes boring straight at me. "Listen and listen good, mister. If you want to keep flying, forget you ever seen us, see. You never took us nowhere. And if you ever come back here, you'll wish you didn't. Got it?"

"Got it," I said, anxious to get away from these screwballs.

I eluded disaster on the takeoff. I was up to speed and poised for getting off the water when I spotted a huge, flat ice cake moving downriver toward me. The house-sized ice slab could rip off the pontoons and send me spinning down the river out of control. I kept full power on and managed to have just enough elevation above the water that the pontoons struck the surface of the ice without colliding. The long ice slab now acted like a ski jump and I got airborne instantly.

All kinds of suspicions about the two men arose in my mind as I climbed out of that bleak canyon and turned the ship's nose toward Fairbanks.

When I checked in at the Wien office after 10 P.M., a note was waiting: "Herm, the FBI wants to see you. They want you to talk to them in Room 238, Nordale, as soon as you get back. Said it's urgent."

After inviting me in, the agents showed me their identification and began questioning me in great detail about my two passengers. For more than forty-five minutes they quizzed me on virtually everything I'd observed about the passengers — their weapons, their luggage, their appearance, their conversations, their clothes and even their attitude.

"They told me to forget I'd ever taken them out there and warned me against coming back," I concluded.

"We can understand that," one of the men said. "Both are dangerous killers on our fugitives list. They'd murder you without blinking if they thought you stood in their way."

The agents also mentioned they believed the fugitives were headed for Russia.

What happened to them? Though I watched the papers carefully after that for any news of their capture, I didn't see anything.

The mystery of the fugitives remains a mystery.

21

TOKLAT ORDEAL

AT 10:15 P.M. ON July 5, 1940, the shrill phone jolted me out of a dream.

"Yeah?" I grumbled sleepily.

Fritz Wien's voice came over the wire. "Hated to wake you, Herm, but we just got an urgent call from Nenana. A trapper on the Toklat River is suffering bad — needs to be evacuated. Appendicitis, maybe. Friend of his hiked in to Nenana to get help. Says the guy's suffering terribly. I said we'd do our best."

The line remained silent for a couple of moments as I rubbed my sleep-dulled eyes.

"Look, Fritz," I groused, asserting my right to gripe and stall, "you're asking me to scout around that river at night to locate a trapper who's out there somewhere and bring him back. How am I gonna find him in the first place? How do I get down and out of that river at night? Anybody think of that?"

Fritz said nothing. He understood I was just revving up to get going, and was probably grabbing for my pants, which I was.

"Okay, Fritz," I said, forcing myself to my feet, still fighting drowsiness. "See you in fifteen minutes."

Fritz was standing in the near-darkness not far from the Cushman Street bridge. He had already yanked out the rear seat in the Fairchild and stowed blankets and pillows aboard, so I could transport the trapper back in a prone position. And he'd gassed the float plane for a three-hour flight.

I got off the Chena at 11 P.M., my flight taking me along the

Kantishna to where it meets the fork of the Toklat. I began groping my way up the Toklat, my eyes straining for some signal from the trapper — a flare, a bonfire, a flashlight, anything.

The meandering Toklat below me was a dimly seen ribbon of silver slicing through fields of darkness. Even with the Midnight Sun in that part of the North it can get pretty dark around midnight, especially in river canyons.

I dropped lower, shuttling back and forth along a five-mile river stretch where I figured the guy might be. The mission kept looking increasingly hopeless. No lights below. No landmarks. No lamplit cabin window — nothing. Maybe the trapper wasn't in this section of the Toklat at all.

Could he be dead? I dismissed that thought instantly, clinging to the conviction that the poor guy *had* to be down there waiting for someone to come and get him. But, assuming he *was* alive, why wasn't he signaling to me in some way? Without some initiative from him, I'd never be able to find him. I'd have to give up.

At best I had less than a half hour to reconnoiter. If I hung around much more, I'd be sticking my neck out. Getting down on the river, getting out and flying eighty-five miles to Fairbanks was going to consume every drop of fuel aboard. Though I was thinking of abandoning the effort, for the sake of my conscience I had to be absolutely sure I'd done everything in my power to get to the trapper.

On what I told myself was going to be my last sweep of the river before retreating, I glimpsed a faint, split-second glimmer in the darkness, something so fleeting it could have been my imagination, or a fish stirring up silver in a dark pool.

Quickly I banked, circled, and moved upstream again toward the place where I thought I'd seen the light.

Now, of course, I had to go down. I dropped toward the river channel, flying slowly upstream, the pontoons skimming the surface of the Toklat by inches. I tried not to think of boulders, snags, overhangs or midstream sandbars that could seize the plane and flip it upside down. Now the bottoms of the pontoons were merging slowly with the river's surface, but the wingtips were narrowly missing bushes and trees on the banks.

I taxied upstream slowly, scanning both banks and praying that pinpoint of light would show again. The river had narrowed dangerously like the center part of an hourglass, and brush on the left bank was hitting the right wing. Bad! In a few moments the river widened again, and I was no longer chopping brush.

I kept swiveling my head, eyes straining. I glanced at my watch. Midnight. This screwball, needle-in-the-haystack business, I griped to myself.

All kinds of doubts began annoying me. Even if the guy wasn't dead, there was no way of being certain that he wasn't in a section of the river other than the one I was searching. And if that was so, how could I possibly find him?

I was thinking of pulling out and returning again in daylight, when I saw the glimmer — no more than a faint spark in the night — against the dark backdrop of the left bank.

My hope and determination renewed, I veered the plane gently to the left until I heard the left float scrape gravel, then cut the switch.

A line in hand, I scrambled out on the float, splashed out into the shallow water, and fastened the pontoon heels to thick brush roots.

"Hey!" I yelled, swinging a flashlight. "Hey!"

Had imagination been playing tricks? Had I *really* seen a light? Forcing my way through thick brush, I kept calling, moving along the bank. Another momentary light flash caught my eye. This time it was less than fifty feet away.

"Here . . . here!" I heard a feeble cry.

Another light flickered briefly. In my flashlight beam I could see a man sprawled in the gravel holding a sputtering match high above his prone body. The sourdough's bearded face in the spotlight was tortured and gaunt, the feverish eyes staring. As a new spasm of pain struck the man, he twisted and his face scraped the dirt.

"Hurts . . ." he moaned softly. "Hurts . . ."

I knelt beside him. "You're gonna be okay, pardner," I assured him. "Have you out in no time."

In his right hand he held a single match and struck it against the rough side of an empty box, pain distorting his face as he watched the match gutter out. "Last match . . ." he said. "Kept lightin' 'em when I heard your plane. Never thought my life would hang on . . . on a coupla siwash matches."

"How long you been here?"

101

"Too long," he said. "Thank God you came. Thought I'd die — tonight. Gave up hope. I'm so damn sick."

"We've got to get out of here," I said. "Plane's close."

I grabbed him under the armpits and lifted him slowly to his feet. He swayed against me weakly, moaning. I winced at how badly he was hurting. Gasping for breath, I dragged him along the bank, his heels plowing twin furrows in the thin gravel.

At the plane I lowered him slowly toward the water's edge, then dragged him to the end of the float, splashing icy water in his face to keep him from passing out.

"Try to help now," I said quietly. "As I start lifting, try to stay on your feet."

"Stay . . . on . . . feet. . . . Stay . . ."

I had him almost to his feet when he moaned and went limp, his sagging body like lead against me.

"We'll try it again, pardner," I told him, admiring his spirit.

"Sorry . . . sick . . . can't . . ."

"That's okay — we'll do it this time. Grab me around the neck — any way you can. That's it." I thought I had him in a firm grip when his hold on my neck weakened, and he toppled backward into the pool alongside the plane. The splash hit me like an electric shock and without knowing exactly how I got there, I found myself thrashing around in the pool, my arms sweeping in a wide arc to grab him. Adrenalin was surging through me as I held him around the shoulders in waist-deep water, and began struggling with him toward the float.

Somehow I got him around the control cables, and moving inch by inch was able to wedge him against the open door. A new spasm of pain struck him. He kept trembling violently and groaning and I knew he was all but unconscious.

"Just about there, pardner," I said. "Keep your legs stiff. Hang on to me till I get you moving backward. Then just let go — fall back. Got it?"

"Try. . . try . . ." he moaned.

As he stood framed from the waist up in the open door, I quickly shifted my weight against him, my fingers anchored in his armpits, forcing the upper part of his body backward. His shoulders moved backward to the floor of the plane.

"You did it!" I praised.

Gasping, I lifted and slid him a couple of feet farther into the plane. Then I got in quickly and dragged him all the way in and onto the blankets Fritz had placed there. I got a pillow under his head and draped a wool blanket over him. I scooted out, untied the line, and got back into the left seat. Now to get the heck off the river in one piece.

Even under daylight conditions, the Toklat is treacherous for float operations. Now I didn't have daylight, didn't have much fuel, and didn't have much time.

The trapper had stopped moaning and lay utterly motionless.

As I roared up the river, it began narrowing rapidly. I was just about on the step, committed at full power, when the damn river swept sharply to the left. I had only seconds to react. Hunched forward tensely, I applied left aileron to bring the right wing up. The right float seemed to be shuddering — then it broke free. Hallelujah!

Escaping the deadly, twisting, boulder-choked Toklat left me limp and trembling. The rosy blush of summer dawn was staining the ridges as I turned the ship to the northeast. Before long the colored lights of Fairbanks and the slow-curving bend of the Chena showed up ahead.

Fritz was waiting and an ambulance was standing by. Fritz, the ambulance driver and I got the poor fellow out of the plane and onto a stretcher. As we carried him to the ambulance, his eyes seemed riveted on mine. Was he trying to thank me?

Fritz looked tired but said nothing. His look told me he understood what it was to challenge the Toklat that night.

Though dead tired and bleary-eyed, I called the hospital before hitting the sack.

"He's in surgery and he's going to pull through," the doctor told me. "But if you hadn't got him here when you did . . ."

I hung up the phone and keeled over on the bed. I was asleep almost before my head hit the pillow.

22

CONSTRUCTION PILOT

ON AUGUST 16, 1941, a telephone call changed the course of my life. It was from Leon B. ("Slim") DeLong, the Anchorage-based superintendent for Morrison-Knudsen (MK), one of the world's largest construction companies, with hundreds of men employed on Alaskan defense projects. The company, with headquarters at Boise, Idaho, had earned a global reputation for getting tough jobs done under the worst possible conditions.

"One of our big problems is getting key people back and forth between our airport construction jobs," he said after introducing himself. "We need a good pilot and can offer you seven hundred dollars a month to start and all your expenses away from home. We'd appreciate your answer — now."

His out-of-the-blue offer startled me. How had DeLong heard about me and how had he sized up my qualifications?

"I really appreciate your offer, Mr. DeLong —" I began.

"Just call me Slim," he interrupted.

"Wien's paying me seven hundred dollars, Slim," I said. "So, if I can't do better —"

"That's too bad," he interrupted again. "Nice talking to you anyhow. Goodbye."

After he hung up abruptly, I wondered whether I'd made a mistake. A half hour later my phone rang again. My next-door neighbor, a telegrapher with the Army Communications System in the federal building, asked me to pick up an important wire that had just arrived. I opened it at the ACS counter.

THIS IS YOUR CONTRACT WITH MK AS EXECUTIVE
PILOT, $800 MONTHLY ALL EXPENSES AWAY FROM
HOME. PROCEED LOS ANGELES NEXT AVAILABLE
PAN AM FLIGHT AND REPORT TO MK BRANCH THERE
TO EVALUATE AIRCRAFT FOR PURCHASE. TICKET AT
PAN AM COUNTER FAIRBANKS TOMORROW MORNING.
WELCOME ABOARD. SLIM DE LONG.

Good Lord! I hadn't accepted any offer, yet Slim had deci-
sively upped the ante, hired me and was already ordering me to Los
Angeles.

Two days later, as I stepped off the Pan Am flight at Seattle's
Boeing Field, I was met by an MK executive who handed me expense
money and credit cards for the fuel I'd be buying while flying MK's
new plane back to Alaska.

"You're the first and only pilot MK has ever hired," one of
the execs at MK's Los Angeles office informed me as we drove to
Burbank airport to get a look at the plane that was for sale.

It was a Howard D.G.A., a designation that stood for Damn
Good Airplane. The sleek 350-horsepower craft had been designed
by a former United pilot working out of Chicago. About forty of the
aircraft had been built.

I flew the plane and was delighted with it.

"They're asking twenty-one thousand dollars, though it sold
for twenty thousand dollars new," I told DeLong when I called him
from the hangar. "Right now, D.G.A.'s are hard to get. My advice is
buy."

"You've just got yourself a new airplane," he said.

Walking back to where the D.G.A. was parked in one of the
hangar stalls, I saw a familiar-looking, heavyset fellow sprawled out
on the floor beneath another D.G.A., right next to mine.

"Haven't I seen you somewhere before?" I asked. I suddenly
realized I had seen him many times before — on the screen of the
Lathrop Theatre.

"You're Wallace Beery," I said, walking up close. Beery just
grunted. "I've seen all your pictures and —"

Beery stopped what he was doing and stared at me, still on
his back. "Sure good to meet you in person, Mr. Beery," I said lamely.

Beery, wearing tattered overalls, his face and hands smeared
with grease and oil, got to his feet and continued to look at me coldly.

"So you've met me," he growled, then slumped back to the concrete floor and crawled back under the airplane.

I headed back to Alaska alone in MK's new plane on August 21, 1941. I had crossed the California-Oregon border and was approaching Grants Pass when the receiver began to crackle. "NC18209 northbound — what's your position?" the Civil Aeronautics Authority controller wanted to know.

I gave the CAA my position and time over Grants Pass.

The CAA acknowledged, then after a slight pause, the controller inquired: "What's your flight plan?"

A long pause. I visualized the en route controllers shaking their heads over this dummkopf who had blundered into their sector. "Your flight plan, sir," the controller explained patiently, "is where you set out from and where you are going."

"Well, I left L.A. at eight this morning and I'm on my way to Seattle."

"Did you file a flight plan before leaving L.A.?"

I squirmed like a crook getting the third degree. "Nobody mentioned a flight plan," I managed. "Sorry."

"What's your cruising speed and how much fuel do you have aboard?"

"My speed — uh — 160. Four and a half hours of fuel remaining."

After a long pause, the controller was back. "We've filed your flight plan to Seattle for you, sir," he said in a tone a prim teacher might use in lecturing a dunce. "In the future, sir, we'd appreciate it if you'd file your en route flight plan *before* departure."

"Thanks, I will," I promised. From then on, I reported my position and time at each station.

The next day I visited MK's Seattle offices, which took up the entire floor of a downtown skyscraper. It was a busy place with phones jangling, typewriters clattering and people rushing around with blueprints and contracts.

I met several executives, including Bob Gebo, an engineer who later flew with me on many occasions, and Fred Craddock, MK's chief bookkeeper, who later transferred to Anchorage. All seemed eager to shake hands with MK's "first pilot."

While I was talking to Gebo, a tall fellow in a rumpled gray suit strolled up looking like someone who had just wandered in off the street.

"Herm, I'd like you to meet —" Gebo began.

"I'm Ray Shinn," the rumpled guy broke in, giving me a firm handclasp. "Can I bum a ride to Juneau with you tomorrow? I'm not a pilot, but I can hand you charts and stuff like that."

"It's all right with me, but what's your job?"

"Clerk," Shinn said and Gebo winced.

"Can you get permission from whoever's the boss around here?" I asked.

"He's got permission," Gebo assured me.

Shinn was out at Boeing Field at the 7 A.M. takeoff time, still wearing his rumpled suit and carrying an overnight bag. As we moved northward, Shinn, seated beside me, kept handing me the appropriate navigation chart from a stack arranged in proper order on a clipboard. During the trip he plied me with questions about all fifty-five hundred hours of my flying time, impressing me as being unusually inquisitive.

After we passed Mount Sheppard and I began my descent into the Juneau airport, Ray turned to me and remarked, "Herm, you've done a magnificent job of navigation — hit Juneau right on the button, though you've never flown this route before."

"Thanks, Ray," I said, pleased.

Slim DeLong and some other MK bosses were waiting out on the ramp. As Ray did the introductions, Slim kept studying me carefully, his gaze cool and penetrating. Then he and Ray walked off to the side for a discussion which, I was sure, would include an assessment of the new pilot.

The foreman of MK's Juneau operations walked over. "I see you brought the big boss with you today," he remarked.

"Big boss? He said he was a clerk!"

The foreman laughed. "Clerk my eye," he said. "He's a vice-president of MK — a big wheel."

"But why did he — ?"

"Oh, Ray's apt to tell you anything. He likes to kid people."

I mentally reviewed my conversation with Ray, hoping I hadn't said anything I shouldn't have.

Ray and Slim came back to the plane, and Slim urged me to

fly on to Fairbanks to spend a night with my family. "We'll get together tomorrow afternoon at the Anchorage Hotel."

I was delighted at the chance to spend some time at home before digging in on my new job. The next morning I was on my way to Anchorage to attend my first MK staff meeting, presided over by Slim.

From that time on, Slim and I were together most of the time, often sharing the same hotel room and eating our meals together. The more I worked with him, the more I liked him. He was highly organized and decisive, a born leader. We grew to trust each other implicitly and became the best of friends.

23

CRISIS AT COLD BAY

NOTHING IN MY BUSH PILOT experience equaled what happened at Cold Bay on November 19, 1941. From the time we got there just before nightfall, Slim DeLong and I were flirting with disaster.

It was less than three weeks before Pearl Harbor, and Alaska was suffering an acute case of the jitters. The Territory's defenses were so pathetic and the rumors of imminent Japanese invasion so persistent, that women and children were being evacuated as quickly as transportation could be arranged. MK and other construction firms were working feverishly under heavy military pressure to bring airfields and other defense installations closer to readiness.

The first enemy blows, it was generally believed, would strike somewhere in the Aleutians, where defense construction work was being pushed at a frantic pace. Nowhere did the threat of enemy attack seem so imminent as at Cold Bay, where airport and other construction proceeded around the clock.

I was surprised when Slim informed me that the landing area at Cold Bay was "ready." His information was based on a garbled message that should have said the landing area was "ready for fill." Actually, completion of Cold Bay airport was still months away. Pending completion of the airfield, supplies and personnel had to be brought in by ship. Only the birds were landing at Cold Bay.

We began our flight to Cold Bay at daybreak on the nineteenth, unaware that there would be no place to land the Howard when we got there. Once we got beyond Port Heiden on the Alaska

Peninsula, the fateful "point of no return" for Aleutian flights, the weather began to turn nasty.

Recurrent rain squalls kept slashing across the windshield. Marauding fog played hide-and-seek with the blurred coastline, gobbling up large chunks of the peninsula, then spitting them out again.

As we moved beyond Port Heiden, our two-thousand-foot visibility and five-mile ceiling dwindled alarmingly. Darkness was approaching as we spotted the jutting crater of 8,215-foot Mount Pavlof, with smoke and ash churning upward from its rim. Though we had enough fuel with a little to spare to get us to Cold Bay, we couldn't do any fooling around once we got there.

After we passed Pavlof, the weather cleared briefly and we got a glimpse of Cold Bay's hook-shaped outline to our left.

Slim's eyeballs were against the window as we skimmed the airfield construction area. He gasped sharply.

"Oh my God, Herm," he said, shocked by what he saw below. "A goddamn mess down there. No runway — no place to land. And they told me —"

The scene below scared me, too. Puddles, lagoons and gravel pits were everywhere in the future landing area. Heavy equipment, piles of lumber and heaps of construction supplies booby-trapped all the open places. I began to sweat.

Murky twilight was merging with approaching darkness and the fuel indicator was hovering near the empty mark.

Though there seemed no way out of our dilemma, my mind kept groping. Could we land on the beach? I swung around and skimmed the beach area up and down for a couple of miles. Landing anywhere along that coast would be suicidal. I had no intention of offering up two human sacrifices to that deadly succession of ravines, coves and cliffs. But we had to go in *somewhere*.

"Okay, Slim," I groused, feeling utterly hopeless and angry at having been painted into this black corner. "MK told us the runway down there was ready. So where does MK want me to land?"

Slim was in no mood for badgering. Angrily he slapped the windshield with the Cold Bay air chart he'd been holding. "Goddamn it, Herm," he lashed out, livid with rage, probably at himself for getting us into this deadly jam, "I don't give a good goddamn *where* you land." Then he retreated into tight-lipped silence.

I instantly regretted my outburst. Though Slim was responsible for our predicament, he hadn't put us there intentionally; I shouldn't have shifted my burden to him. Getting back to earth was clearly my problem, not his.

I clamped a hand on his shoulder. "Slim," I said, "I'm sorry and I apologize." Our eyes met and his expression softened.

"What in the hell *are* we going to do?" he asked.

"I'm not sure, Slim. Anything we do will be risky. And we don't have enough fuel to dilly-dally. I've got to bite the bullet — now."

"Is it the construction area?"

"There's nowhere else, no other way, Slim." But the thought of trying to land on that torn-up construction site was frightening. If the gear hit a two-by-four, a boulder, anything at all, the tail would whip up and we'd pancake into the mud upside down, an awful way to be entombed.

A miserable squall was raking the field, and hundreds of tiny rain droplets fanned out across the windshield like bursts of quicksilver. The time had come.

"Okay, Slim," I said, cranking the stabilizer tabs down and setting the prop in low pitch. "We're going down. I'll try to get us down close as I can to those workers. If we flip, maybe they'll be able to get to us. Be sure your seat belt's tight. Brace your feet tight against the floor. Brace your hands on the instrument panel. When we hit, cushion your head with your hands."

If the Old Reaper was lurking around — and I strongly suspected he was — he must have been grinning out of his skull.

As we descended I fought to stay calm, focus my mind on the landing. My thoughts were going a mile a minute.

Aim straight at that gang. Touch down maybe a hundred feet from them. Stall. Let the wheels brush the surface, then begin applying full power. Now! Drop it down!

My heart was in my throat and sweat poured off me as the wheels began to sink in. Then panic seized me. The wheels weren't digging in evenly and the gear was beginning to slice into the gumbo at a crazy angle. If I continued, it was going to be a rotten, loused-up — and tragic — landing. I aborted the landing, pouring on three-quarters power and feeling the ship shudder and tremble as it tore loose from the surface. We were airborne again, the left wing dipping

113

steeply as we wheeled over the gaping, hard-hatted construction stiffs clustered below. One guy clamped both his hands over his eyes. Others stood staring at us, motionless and open-mouthed.

"Goofed that one," I yelled to Slim, who was pale and silent. "I'll get it right the second time."

I glanced at the gas gauge. Empty. I prayed there was enough left to get us around the field just once.

Now, in utter twilight, we were at our starting point again. I lined the plane up and aimed at the cluster of workers the best I could. Good, bad or indifferent, I was going to go in now. It was getting too dark and the fuel was too low to hope for a third chance.

Again we were skimming the surface of the construction site. This time I kept the plane headed a bit to the left of where I'd touched down earlier.

Now!

We smacked the surface harder than last time, but both wheels made contact at perfect right angles to the surface. As a whirlpool of mud began swirling and churning beneath us, I poured on power, delighted to find some left. We sank rapidly in the gumbo, still moving forward as speed bled off. I kept the last of our power blasting to keep the nose from digging in as torrents of mud boiled around the underside of the plane.

So far, no obstacles, thank God. No two-by-fours, no boulders. We had decelerated so fast my seat belt smashed at my belly like a boxer's blow. The power conked out but we didn't need it anymore — we had come to a standstill. In one piece. Upright. Alive. Not a scratch on either of us.

"Hallelujah!" Slim yelled jubilantly. "You Norwegian son of a gun — you got us down!"

We were both full of the joy of just being alive.

A rugged, bearded guy driving a big cat plowed through yard-deep mud to reach us. He turned out to be the MK boss at Cold Bay and he gave us a hand as we transferred to his vehicle.

"Man, what a landing!" he exclaimed, pumping my hand. "We figured any pilot who'd try a landing like that had to be either damn crazy or damn good!"

"Herm's the best pilot this side of the moon," Slim said.

"Just the luckiest," I said.

The hard-hats hauled a large plank skid out to the plane,

then with ropes and bulldozer got the plane up on the skid and over to shore.

Weather marooned us at Cold Bay for four long days. While Slim conferred with MK people, I busied myself with the prop, filing off numerous rough spots, nicks and indentations. Those four days of howling wind, unrelieved bleakness and stinging rain seemed never-ending. Now I wanted out. For four days I had been studying the straight, narrow road leading to the radio range. I measured it and found there would be only a bit more than a foot of space on each side of the wheels if I tried to use the road to take off. If it was all right with Slim I wanted to risk it, though the road was ridiculously narrow.

He was willing. "I've been looking at that road, too," he said. "For four days."

There was another reason Slim was eager to get out of Cold Bay. He confided in me that military intelligence considered an enemy attack on Alaska imminent.

"We're not doing our country or MK any good marooned out here, Herm. We've got to get back to Anchorage."

"Okay, boss," I told him, "but it's going to be ticklish."

He grinned. "I'm getting used to that," he said.

An Anchorage-bound construction worker boarded, so we weren't as light as I would have liked for such a skittish takeoff.

I managed to generate enough speed to lift the tail and get a clear view of the road ahead. With half the camp as spectators, I accelerated at low pitch and full power, zipped up that narrow road and somehow kept the wheels from straying over the abrupt road edge. If the wheel went over it would put us in the ditch and crack hell out of the plane, to say nothing about what it might do to us.

My mouth was pretty dry by the time we got off.

"We're committed to Naknek," I told Slim as we gained altitude. "There's no way we can try to land on that road and I'm sure not going to land on that field again."

"I'm with you there," Slim said.

We were passing Mount Pavlof when an ominous glaze on the struts and windshield caught my eye. Ice. There's nothing a pilot dreads more than icing. When the stuff begins to build up, the plane's airworthiness deteriorates. Unless you get rid of it, you're in for a forced landing. Where we were flying, there was no place to land.

Ice kept building up alarmingly as we plowed through a thirty-two-degree rain. I veered off some twenty miles to sea and then descended to five hundred feet in search of a warmer area. It worked. The ice glaze crumbled and fell.

Another problem began to bug me. I could get seven hours out of the 135 gallons of fuel aboard. My calculations indicated we'd need at least seven hours of fuel to get to Naknek. My dogleg to get rid of the ice had depleted the fuel reserve I needed. I wasn't going to tell Slim about it unless it looked as if we weren't going to make it. Meanwhile, I was the only one who would be worrying about it.

While passing Egegik on our left, I began feeling anxious as the needle on the fuel gauge trembled uncomfortably close to empty. I tried not to stare at the dial as we crossed over the King Salmon River. Naknek airport was visible just ahead. It was going to be close, a photo finish, maybe.

I throttled back, got the nose down, and began a gentle glide toward the runway that looked a long way off. In seconds we were over the threshold and the wheels were touching down. Whew! I taxied along almost half the runway's mile-long length before the engine gasped its last, then let momentum carry us off to the side.

"Why in hell can't we taxi to the mess hall?" Slim demanded.

"Sorry Slim," I said. "We're going to have to hoof it. Ran out of gas."

"Just this minute?"

"Yeah."

Slim just shook his head.

We were enjoying a steak dinner at the mess hall when an MK official walked over to chat with Slim.

"Any reports from Anchorage?" Slim asked.

"None," said the official. "Anchorage is off the air — blacked out."

That startled me, but Slim didn't look surprised.

"There were reports a strange aircraft had penetrated the area," the MK guy continued. "Scared hell out of everybody in Anchorage. The military's on full alert. All kinds of invasion rumors buzzing around."

Slim got to his feet abruptly. "Figure you can get into Anchorage even though it's blacked out?" he asked.

"Sure, unless some trigger-happy fighter pilots at Fort

Richardson decide to shoot us down." I had reason to remember that remark later.

On our flight to Anchorage, I followed Cook Inlet's shoreline and was glad to see Fire Island beneath us. For me it had been a long, miserable, thoroughly upsetting trip.

I throttled back, put the prop in low pitch, and slowed to a hundred miles an hour, asking my passengers to keep their eyes peeled for a crucial landmark — George Lingo's large, two-story house on a bluff at the west edge of town.

Everybody spotted it at once. With that point of reference, it would be easy to get into Merrill Field.

As we skimmed low over the Federal Building, then sidled over to Sixth Avenue, which led directly to Merrill Field, we didn't see a light anywhere. In a few moments the wheels were touching down on the west end of the runway.

The next morning I went out to Merrill Field and joined the crew of mechanics checking the airplane. A big, rawboned G.I. walked over and called me aside. Speaking in a Southern accent, he told me he was one of the two Fort Richardson soldiers assigned to man two .50-caliber machine guns at the west end of the field.

"Were you-all the pilot who flew in here last night just after ten?" he asked.

"That was me."

He extended his hand. "Mister, you made a fantastic landing in the dark. But you almost got yourself killed."

"I did?"

"Yeah. My buddy and I had orders to fire at anything that looked like an enemy plane, and for a while, you did. We heard you approaching from the west, slow and easy and right in the groove for landing. You were so close we could see the blue flames shooting out of the exhaust. We had our fingers on the triggers and were about to blast away when I got to thinking. 'Hey, don't shoot!' I yelled to my buddy. 'Anybody making that kind of approach at night must have flown in here lots of times, so he's friendly.' "

"And that's why you didn't shoot me down?"

"That's why, mister."

"You did some real smart thinking last night, soldier," I said.

"Yes sir," he replied, beaming. "That's what saved you. That's what kept us from blasting you to kingdom come."

24

THE ENEMY STRIKES

On December 7, 1941, I was in the mess hall at Cold Bay when I heard a fighter pilot remark: "If the Japs had any idea how rotten Alaska's defenses are, they'd have invaded long ago."

His words gave me a chill that wasn't eased when news of the Pearl Harbor attack came over the radio.

The shock waves penetrated to the tiniest Eskimo village.

Dense fog kept Slim and me from leaving Cold Bay until December 9.

I was glad to get back to Anchorage. The town's citizens were having a tough time adjusting to war. Rumor, fear and even panic seemed to have captured the town. False reports terrified the populace. One rumor had it that the entire West Coast had come under heavy Japanese attack and Japanese invasion forces were landing on Alaskan beaches. Honey-voiced Tokyo Rose, in broadcasts beamed at Alaska, eagerly fanned such rumors to stir up as much hysteria as possible. Trying to find out what was actually going on was next to impossible because, initially, all radio transmissions were banned. The misinformation peddled by Tokyo Rose came through loud and clear. Fearful Alaska residents were left totally and literally in the dark as blackouts were strictly enforced. In this atmosphere of turmoil, Alaska swiftly took on wartime footing.

On December 10, I flew to Naknek with Bob Gebo and Orval Tosch. Dense fog grounded us there for two days. Everybody in Naknek was still feeling the aftermath of Pearl Harbor. As in Anchorage, false rumors were rife. Mess hall and barracks windows were painted black to keep even the faintest light from providing any guidance to the pilots of enemy bombers and fighters. Naknek was an eerie, frightened place in the dense fog, which had shut the airport down tight.

Feeling somewhat secure in fog so thick it was sure to discourage an enemy attack, Gebo, Tosch and I wandered out on the runway after dinner. I carried our only weapon, a .251 Newton rifle. It was calm and quiet and so foggy we could see only a few feet ahead of us.

Suddenly the roar of an aircraft engine in the sky above us paralyzed us in our tracks.

"Jap airplane!" Gebo yelled, his voice shaky. "Has to be! Nobody else would fly in weather like this!"

I heard Tosch scream as the roar grew deafening, "Let's get the hell out of here!"

We heard the plane circling then heading back toward us again. I was expecting bursts of machine-gun fire or racks of bombs at any instant. The plane's roar indicated it was moving down the centerline of the runway, at a very low altitude.

Adrenalin gave top speed to three pairs of feet as we veered off the runway at a tangent and zoomed across a five-foot ditch alongside the runway.

Again we heard the aircraft's deafening roar overhead. The plane seemed to be skimming the runway as we beelined toward the mess hall.

For some reason I flipped the rifle to Gebo, who caught it deftly.

"Goddamit, Herm," Gebo exploded, still running as fast as he could. "I don't need that thing — it's slowing me down. You brought it. Here — take it." He flipped the rifle back to me on the run, like a football being passed back and forth. I caught it and kept moving as fast as I've moved in my life.

Though we never found out for sure, there were indications that a carrier-based Japanese fighter plane may have locked into Naknek's radio navigation beam, and had homed in on one leg of our low-frequency station. This would have guided the pilot right down the runway centerline, where we heard him coming in. The military assured us that no friendly aircraft had ventured out into the fog that night.

The next day, we checked our footprints at both sides of the ditch to see how far we had jumped. The footprints were clearly visible on both sides of the ditch and there were no prints at the bottom. Unfortunately I didn't measure the distance, but in our mad dash to get off the field we must have been airborne for a record or near-record distance.

■ ■ ■

After Pearl Harbor, the military took over operation of most airlines in Alaska and grounded most light-plane operations. Even the Alaska Railroad and the movement of trucks and buses were placed under military control.

The coming of war to Alaska intensified Slim DeLong's efforts. He added several hours to his work day and pushed himself to the brink of exhaustion.

Slim's never-ending quest for perfection, his unslakable thirst for accomplishment and his ravenous appetite for hard work became all the more evident. Very early, Slim's remarkable personal qualities won my respect, admiration and friendship. Though hard-driving, strictly business and tough as nails, he had a heart of gold.

Every couple of weeks he'd insist I take "leave" and head for Fairbanks to spend a couple of days with my family. On December 24, 1941, though burdened by an almost intolerably heavy wartime workload, Slim insisted I return to Fairbanks to spend the holidays at home, "war or no war."

"We'll survive without you until after New Year's," he assured me. "I don't want you coming back the day after Christmas."

As Slim was sure I would, I showed up back in Anchorage the day after Christmas. He chuckled as he handed me a heavy schedule of year-end flights worked out during my one-day absence. In many respects, Slim and I were two of a kind. Despite occasional rough times in our relationship, my deep regard for him never diminished.

Pearl Harbor brought new importance to the word "priority." You needed "priority" to fly on an airline. You needed "priority" to leave Alaska or go to it. You needed "priority" to purchase fuel and lots of other things.

Those not essential to Alaska's war effort were encouraged to leave. Many Alaskans didn't need much encouragement after Tokyo Rose spread the rumor that America's military considered

Alaska "expendable" and was willing to sacrifice the Territory to buy time for the main battle against the Japanese.

"Herm," Slim told me one day, "we've got to get your family out of Alaska while I'm still able to get you air transportation priority."

"Where can I send them?"

"Where do you want them to go?"

"The best place would probably be my wife's folks in Virginia, Minnesota," I said.

"That's it, then," he said with finality. He immediately arranged for the priority needed to purchase airline tickets to Seattle and railroad tickets for the remainder of the trip.

I spent the next two days preparing for the family's flight south. Saddened by enforced separation from my loved ones, I nevertheless realized that others were making far greater sacrifices.

The war had come home to me in a very personal way.

25

VOLCANO LANDING

THE MORE I STUDIED Aniakchak Volcano from the air, the more I became convinced that the landing Slim wanted me to attempt would be far too dangerous.

The volcano's steep terrain resembled a scuffed-up gray bedsheet. Ravines and gullies of uncertain depth wrinkled the ancient fire-belcher's surface everywhere. A nightmare of obstacles would confront me, I was sure, if I made the foolhardy attempt to touch down.

I had no desire to challenge Aniakchak.

In the frenzy of wartime reaction to the enemy invasion threat, the military was considering the possibility of constructing secret installations in the shadow of the volcano. They needed precise, on-site data and asked for DeLong's help.

In discussing the matter at the Anchorage hotel the day before our flight to Aniakchak, Slim emphasized the urgency of the military's request. "It should be possible for us to get down somewhere in this area," he said, jabbing a pencil at a section of the volcano he had highlighted by enclosing it in a red-outlined rectangle on an aerial photo.

"Seems too torn up and steep to me," I said.

He jabbed a pencil at the photo again. "Maybe you can get in here on the north slope. Far less vegetation and it's less than a mile from the place the brass wants us to look at."

I had landed on mountaintops, gravel bars and moose pastures, but I had never landed on a volcano and had no eagerness to attempt it now. But curbing Slim's persistence wasn't going to be easy.

"I'd have to be convinced it was feasible before I risked it," I insisted.

"Look, Herm," he said, "The Army wants us to evaluate that site right away so some construction decisions vital to the defense effort can be made. It's wartime and we've got to adjust our thinking to taking wartime risks."

"All I'm saying," I told him, "is that it doesn't look good to me. I'll give it another look from the air."

"Herm, you've flown in and out of all kinds of tight places without getting anybody killed. I'm confident you'll be able to pull this landing off, too."

I refused to budge from a position I've always held — the go-or-no-go decision must be the pilot's.

We left Anchorage for the flight to Aniakchak in the pre-dawn darkness on January 11, 1942. Bob Gebo was along to assist Slim in conducting studies at the site — if I could ever get them there.

The chilling prospect haunted me all the way to the mountain. The very thought of it filled me with foreboding. For one thing, the D.G.A., the fastest aircraft in commercial use in Alaska at the time, was far too fast for that kind of operation. For a volcano landing you need a plane that can settle in eagle-slow and stop quickly.

Our first orbit of the volcano did nothing to dispel my apprehension. From a pilot's standpoint, I found the ugly, broken terrain below repellent.

"Any chance?" Slim asked.

"None that I've seen so far, Slim, especially with a fast plane like ours."

Slim retreated into grouchy silence. Even so, I had reached the fairly firm conclusion that the only way Slim was going to get down on that volcano was to use a parachute.

We were beginning our fifth circuit of the peak when something on the north slope caught my attention — a relatively smooth, bare patch of mountain just above its base. I began reconsidering.

I nudged Slim and pointed to the area, which was just a couple of miles from the section Slim had marked on the aerial photo.

Slim's scowl vanished instantly. Eagerly he studied the area. "Looks great," he said enthusiastically. "Let's go."

Repeated fly-bys convinced me we could probably get in okay. A slope that steep would bleed off landing speed rapidly. The big question was the gear. I had to assume it wouldn't get ripped off somewhere on the mountain. I knew if I set down at the wrong angle all kinds of unhealthy things could result.

All keyed up now, I cranked the elevator tabs down, flattened the prop, and began settling toward the slope. The terrain below began giving me second thoughts. Had I misjudged?

Beneath the wings, the volcano's corrugated surface began to blur. I hauled back on the wheel and cut the throttle. The tail wheel began digging sharply into the surface as the plane melded into the uphill slope. A terrible racket resulted — a violent shuddering and trembling as dense ponytails of volcanic debris spewed upward and volleys of pebbles spattered the fuselage like intermittent machine-gun fire.

I winced as we skirted a pyramidal collection of rocks the gear just missed. We thudded into and out of shallow potholes, then staggered through ankle-deep depressions in the pitted surface.

The gear was taking a terrible beating as I fought to keep the plane straight, constantly maneuvering, correcting, steadying the unruly beast, calling on every flying instinct at my command. I kept bracing for the next jarring blow that would whip the gear out from under us. Yet somehow that tremendously sturdy, flexible assembly survived all the shocks and punishment the volcano could dish out.

We began to slow, and stopped less than fifty feet from a pie-shaped wedge of slope gouged from the mountain by a giant landslide or earthquake. The dropoff near us was something to shudder about.

I felt limp. I was drenched with perspiration, drained of energy.

"Helluva landing!" Gebo yelled.

"Tremendous!" Slim said jubilantly.

I was afraid of what I might retort so I kept my lips buttoned. My hands were still trembling and I was trying to simmer down from the incredible pressure and strain.

Slim and Gebo kept chatting nonchalantly, chortling and laughing as they got their gear together. I found their bantering somehow annoying. Apparently they had already dismissed the peril of that landing. Maybe it was better that they remained blissfully unaware of what it entailed.

"We'll be gone for about six hours," Slim told me. "Expect we'll have any trouble getting off?"

"Hard to tell," I said. "I'll give the terrain a close once-over while you're gone."

After they trudged away I lay back against the slope, leaning on my elbows. I shuddered at the thought of the amount of work I'd have to do to make the gullied, pitted surface below relatively safe for takeoff. And I had just six hours.

With an eight-foot stick I measured out a departure zone sixteen feet wide and a thousand feet long. I figured I could convert the two extra five-gallon cans of gas stowed in the baggage compartment to shovels. I poured the fuel into the tank, then used my hatchet to slash off about half of the front part of each can, leaving the handles in place. I began using the cans to level countless rain-gouged ruts, miniature ridges and irregular outcrops of dirt and rock.

I tore into loose tangles of dead brush and dragged boulders off to the side of the "runway." I would work doggedly for about an hour, then, thoroughly exhausted, sprawl out on the dirt until a semblance of strength returned. Then I would stagger up and attack the terrain again. Hour after hour I toiled to smooth out that narrow section of volcano. Muscles and bones ached, blisters sprouted and bled on gloveless hands, throbbing pain tortured my back and shoulders. I forced myself to keep fighting the irregularities on that infernal slope, working as if my life depended on it — as it probably did.

Those were six hours of the toughest labor I've ever performed. I had to do it. Before it was over, both tin-can shovels were reduced to twisted shards of bright metal. I collapsed from weariness — dirty, gasping, bleeding, beat-up and irritable.

I forced myself to perform one more task before I quit. I staggered to the far end of the "runway" with the remains of the shovels and placed the two chunks of bright metal side by side to sight on when I began my down-slope departure.

Slim and Gebo came back around 5 P.M. thoroughly pooped. Slim studied my runway improvement project with the practiced eye of a construction boss.

"Not bad, Herm," he said.

After they stowed away their equipment we got into the plane, cinched our seat belts and were ready to go. All of us were too tired to feel any apprehension about the takeoff.

The trusty D.G.A. — the plane that was far too fast for a volcano landing — now was poised for swooping downhill to get us off that blankety-blank volcano.

I unlocked the left brake, gunned the engine and wheeled the plane around to the right, its nose pointed at the gas cans far below. I checked the mags and cranked the elevator tabs back to neutral, then turned the engine up to twenty-four hundred RPMs.

Now, accelerating swiftly as we dropped, we began roaring down the formerly unassailable peak. My tireless labor to smooth the upper portion of the takeoff area paid off: we swooped off the volcano using less than half the area I'd labored on.

As the ominous cone dropped away below, I felt a pleasant surge of lightheartedness and shucked all the concerns that had haunted me so persistently since we had left Anchorage.

At the MK mess hall in Naknek we enjoyed a gourmet steak dinner, during which the MK brass crowded around to hear Slim deliver a description of our volcano adventure. We spent that night at Naknek and I enjoyed more than eight hours of snoring good rest. I'd earned that many times over on that miserable mountain.

It always irked me a little that, after all our efforts, the military decided to do nothing with the site.

Over the ensuing years, that volcano landing and takeoff were relived many times in my memory and a time or two in my nightmares.

26

CLASH WITH SLIM

SLIM DELONG'S TOUGH, no-nonsense side emerged whenever he encountered inefficiency or inadequacy. When people didn't move, Slim moved them, and if they still didn't move, he fired them.

Though I felt in no danger of being fired, I became aware early in the winter of 1942 that Slim was casting a jaundiced eye on my flight performance. He was looking for improvement in MK's flight operations, more specifically in the capabilities of one Herm Lerdahl.

Slim never expressed such misgivings openly until after an aborted trip to Naknek. My failure to complete a trip because of weather was plainly a source of frustration to him. He still wasn't as convinced as I was that you can get yourself buried by ignoring the weather. It seemed to irk him that airline pilots got to their destinations in weather that forced light-plane pilots to turn around.

When he had his heart set on getting to one of the jobs, he hated it when I had to turn back. And that's what I had to do on the trip to Naknek.

Even before we left, I urged him to postpone the trip because of the forecasts.

"No way," Slim blustered. "We can always turn back later if it looks bad. Besides, I've *got* to get to Naknek."

Noel Wien had warned me about the deadly flying disease, "get-there-itis." But it wouldn't hurt to check Lake Clark Pass before deciding.

Inner warning alarms clanged in my mind as we entered the approach to the pass. Dense clouds were beginning to move in, threatening to shut the pass drum-tight.

"It's no use, Slim," I said. "We'd be sticking our necks out a mile."

"Hell, Herm," he countered, visibly annoyed, "I can see all the way through to the other side."

"I hear what you're saying, Slim, but I honestly don't think it would be safe." I did a 180.

We rode all the way back to Anchorage in awkward silence. He seemed terribly out of sorts, as if I had somehow conspired with the weatherman to thwart him.

His grumpiness persisted through the dinner hour, when he finally gave vent to his feelings.

"Herm," he declared, "this business of turning around every time the weather's not just right is for the birds. We've got to do something about it. Airline pilots get through all the time. In my opinion, our vital operations are being hampered because you're far too dependent on the weather."

I began to choke up. I felt demeaned and wounded. I felt he had assaulted my professionalism. Hurt and resentful, I reacted in absolutely the wrong way, emotionally.

"Look, Slim," I snapped, slapping my napkin down and getting to my feet, "if you feel you can find another pilot who suits you better, do it. I've had it with your lectures."

Slim also got to his feet, seeming genuinely stunned by my outburst. "Come on now, Herm," he said earnestly, "there's no reason for you to get so hot under the collar. I didn't say anything about getting another pilot."

"But you —"

"Now, listen, Herm. I've always considered you an outstanding pilot. I don't have to be sold on your proficiency. You're exceptionally good, but you can be better. I was getting around to suggesting that instrument training might be helpful to you, and to us, because of the kind of weather we've got to fly in."

Fully cooled down now, I was red-faced at having spouted off in such a juvenile manner.

"Sorry I blew up, Slim," I said.

"I understand perfectly," Slim said. "Let's finish our coffee."

"So you think I need instrument training?" I asked.

"That's right," he said. "MK's sending you to a top-notch instrument school in Dallas. We'll pick up the tab for your training and pay your regular salary. Your job will be waiting when you get back."

"When do I go?"

"You're booked through to Dallas on the January 20 after-noon flight."

I couldn't keep from grinning. It was all so typical of Slim — making careful decisions and then seeing that they're carried out in the least possible time.

As we left the restaurant he remarked, "Herm, I want you to know that, besides being fully satisfied with you as an employee, I consider you a good friend."

The next day I learned that Slim, again typically, had already hired my temporary replacement.

"I'd be glad to brief the new guy on the way the D.G.A. handles," I said. "It has a couple of quirks he ought to know about."

"Good idea. I'll let him know right away."

The next day Slim told me the new pilot had indignantly rejected my offer to help. Slim quoted him as saying, "I can fly anything Lerdahl can — and better."

About a week after I began instrument training in Dallas, I got a letter from Slim indicating that maybe the guy wasn't such a hotshot pilot after all.

"I'm sorry to report," Slim wrote, "that the pilot we hired isn't working for MK anymore. On his first flight, as we were landing at Cordova in perfect weather, he put the plane over on its back. It caught fire, exploded and burned, and Fred, I and the pilot just barely made it out. It scared the holy bejayzus out of us. When I think of all the safe landings you've made under impossible conditions — well, you can't get back soon enough to suit us."

I applied myself diligently to instrument classes, learning how to fly using airspeed and turn-and-bank indicators rather than "seat of the pants." I passed the written tests, and on March 22, 1942, passed the three-hour instrument flight test aloft.

When I got back to Anchorage with my instrument rating, Slim greeted me with a congratulatory handshake and roared when I told him, "I still reserve the right to head back any time I feel like it."

At the time, Jack Jefford, chief pilot for the Civil Aeronautics Authority, was Alaska's only instrument-rated pilot. I became number two.

A couple of weeks later Slim asked me to fly to Cincinnati to look over a ten-place, single-engine Vultee to replace the ill-fated D.G.A. The ship was a powerful 1000-horsepower low-wing job with retractable landing gear, owned by National Sodium Products, Ltd. I bought it for MK. Before I flew it back to Alaska the *Cincinnati Inquirer* ran a story about the transaction, with a picture of me standing with the mayor of Cincinnati, James G. Stewart, and the president of the firm we'd bought the plane from, Allison Bishopric.

The wife of an MK employee, Mrs. Richard Conway, and the Conways' small child were my passengers on the flight back to Alaska.

Slim and other MK officials were at Merrill Field to welcome me back and inspect the new aircraft.

On May 25, Burleigh Putnam of the CAA joined me in the Vultee for a weight-rating flight. He checked me out on stalls and turns, with and without flaps, before giving me his seal of approval. I was now officially rated and qualified to fly passengers in the Vultee.

27

BUSH PILOT AT WAR

ON JUNE 3, 1942, fifteen Japanese attack planes from the carriers *Junyo* and *Rynjo* began a merciless twenty-minute pounding of Dutch Harbor on Unalaska Island in the Aleutian Chain, and repeated the attacks the next day. Seventy-eight Americans were killed and fourteen U.S. planes lost in the two-day assault. On June 7, Japanese troops stormed ashore at Attu and Kiska. Cold Bay was expected to be hit next.

Flying into Cold Bay after the attacks made me uneasy. MK's new Vultee could easily be mistaken for a Japanese fighter and the huge Stars and Stripes painted on each wing and both sides of the fuselage could be overlooked, especially at night. The plane would be a sitting duck, not only for enemy combat pilots but for trigger-happy U.S. fliers.

Cold Bay was bristling with antiaircraft guns and fighter planes. A base that had been defenseless up to a year ago was now a hornet's nest.

As I came in for my approach from the north, I saw two Army P-40s zooming up off the main runway directly toward me. They whizzed past me on either side and I was glad to see they didn't have me in mind.

The Cold Bay operations building was in a whirlwind of excitement. I was told that several Japanese fighter planes had been shot down just a few hours earlier. It was rumored that some Japanese prisoners had been taken.

I had gone to Cold Bay to pick up fourteen construction

workers and fly them to Naknek, where they were needed badly on a project.

They lost no time in scrambling aboard with their bulky toolboxes. Other workers who wanted to get the hell out tried to push their way into the plane and had to be stopped. There wasn't enough room even for fourteen men in the ten-place Vultee, but they had to be stuffed aboard because they were desperately needed at Naknek.

My new passengers were obviously eager to get out before the anticipated attack. "Cold Bay's hanging by a thread," one of them told me. "It's going to get hit hard — and soon." What Slim had told me in confidence indicated that the military felt the same way. Slim also told me the military suspected there was at least one enemy agent among the construction workers at Cold Bay, and that some employees were suspected of trying to get military information out to the wrong people.

"If anyone asks you to take mail out for them, Herm, don't touch it with a ten-foot pole," he warned. "Refer them to the Army Post Office (APO)."

Slim seemed to thrive on the feverish new atmosphere of wartime crisis. There were times he worked almost around the clock to get men and materials to essential projects, and to keep the projects themselves on schedule.

He had an important role in supervising construction of the defenses at Cold Bay and other key points in the Aleutians. MK forces took part in the construction of a 6,000-foot runway at McGrath and a 10,000-foot strip at Nabesna. Smaller fields were built at Bethel and Aniak. Though Alaska was far from fully prepared when the blow struck, carpenters, heavy equipment operators, laborers, plumbers and electricians — and members of the other trades — were essential "troops" in Alaska's defense picture. The role played by Slim and other construction leaders can't be overvalued.

During these hectic, menace-filled days and nights, Slim ran me ragged hopping from one MK project to another at all hours of the day and night. My log for the period after war broke out showed I flew six days a week from early morning until late at night. The routine of each weary day was the same — fly, eat and sleep. I felt a sense of pride in being able to render this vital service at a time when air transportation was so essential to the war effort. Dutch Harbor,

Attu and Kiska had thoroughly shattered any complacency Alaskans might have felt. I was glad my family was safely in Minnesota.

Alaska's bush pilots did yeoman duty in those troubled times. To rush work on the Nabesna airport, MK organized a fast-moving, coordinated "bush pilot cargo airlift." The construction firm's appeal for help in getting equipment and supplies to the site brought pilots to Nabesna from every corner of Alaska. For the first time, a virtual "Who's Who" of Alaska bush pilots were working together on a single project. They were a motley crew of rebels and individualists, accustomed to fighting each other tooth and nail. Now, however, they were working together smoothly and efficiently, sharing the same bunkhouses and mess halls and even, occasionally, finding a kind word for one another.

The dawn-to-dark cargo haul to Nabesna continued without slackening for twenty-three hectic days beginning August 5. Among the bush pilots who participated were Merle K. (Mudhole) Smith, who came up from Cordova; John Walatka and Jack Scavenius from Anchorage; and Rudy Billberg, Frank Barr, Don Emmons and Frank Cramer from Fairbanks, to name just a few.

Each of us made at least eight round trips a day in the hectic scramble to get cargo to Nabesna, most of it moving through Northway. We hung around the Northway mess hall for snacks and coffee while crews refueled our planes and loaded cargo. Our big meal always came after we finished flying for the day and it was dark. We flew with minimum fuel to allow maximum payload. Most of us completed at least one round trip before breakfast.

These pilots put their lives on the line to get vital cargo through. One trip made by Mudhole scared all of us who were watching him take off. The MK mechanics had cut open the fuselage of a Boeing tri-motor to insert a 6,000-gallon oil tank. Crews stacked hundred-pound resin sacks in the front baggage compartment to offset the heavy overload in the center on the ship. It was just too heavy a load.

As a crowd of bush pilots watched, the lumbering, over-loaded Boeing began its staggering takeoff run from Northway. The old beast was trembling and shuddering so badly that every time the plane's tires hit a bump, we could see the fabric wrinkling on the fuselage. There wasn't one of us who wasn't "feeling for" Mudhole as he battled to get that impossible load airborne. We knew he was sweating and maybe praying; it was only after virtually all the runway had been used that he got the Boeing off the ground.

The curtain on my own role in the airlift rang down in dramatic fashion. I was flying five barrels of oil and lots of resin from Nabesna to Northway when it happened.

Ten minutes out of Northway, the top cylinder on the Hornet engine began to dance wildly. It cut out intermittently, then roared back to life, its "burping" producing a roller-coaster flight path.

I was a thousand feet from the west end of the Northway runway, flying over one of the swampy lagoons on the Tanana Flats.

I had the throttle wide open when the Hornet engine quit again. I put the Pilgrim's nose down, hoping I might be able to grease it in on its belly somewhere in the swamp, hoping it wouldn't flip over on its back when it hit.

Suddenly the cantankerous engine coughed a couple of times, then sputtered back to life, churning out full power for the few precious moments I needed to cheat the swamp. Ahead were some trees edging the runway and the power surge provided barely enough altitude to clear the branches. Then the damn thing cut dead again.

I made a steep right turn, diving for the runway to salvage airspeed, and got her down just twenty-five feet from the threshold with a dead engine. I managed to roll free of the runway area by braking on one wheel.

The spectacular landing was witnessed by a Northwest DC-3 crew waiting to take off. Later one of the crew members told me, "I couldn't believe my eyes. Saw you come in over the swamp and begin doing chandelles. First time I ever saw anybody land here like that."

Northway mechanics traced the problem to a broken cylinder that ruptured the manifold intake.

Early in June MK purchased a Spartan, a fast, clean silver bird that we decorated liberally with the American flag to keep it from being mistaken for the enemy.

A hair-raising problem with the Spartan developed on a flight to Anchorage from McGrath with Fred Craddock, another MK official, as my passenger.

Aware that the plane's Wasp engine had been operating too many hours since its last overhaul, I took out a kind of insurance.

136

Since we would be flying over the Alaska Range after dark, I made it a point to get as high as possible in case the engine acted up.

With no oxygen aboard, I had to level out at sixteen thousand feet near the halfway point between McGrath and Anchorage. Suddenly cascades of sparks like those from Fourth of July sparklers began shooting out of the engine. I was puzzled. The dials didn't show anything out of whack but, though we were maintaining an airspeed of 180, we were gradually losing altitude.

Craddock looked scared. "Are we going to make it?" he asked anxiously.

"I hope so. We ought to be able to get in to Merrill or Elmendorf." I didn't want to scare him, and at the same time didn't want to minimize our predicament.

By the time we reached the inlet we were down to a thousand feet, and I was glad to see downtown Anchorage under my wings. We had been dropping about twelve hundred feet per minute, and it seemed certain now that either we were going to make it to Merrill, or Anchorage residents were going to witness a spectacular spark-shooting display from an aircraft attempting to land on Sixth Avenue. We made it to Merrill, coming in at around eighty-five miles per hour with virtually all the engine's "oomph" dissipated. I had just enough power to get me across the west threshold, where I made a shaky landing.

The next day the mechanic working on the engine turned to me, shaking his head. "Intake manifold's burned to hell. Engine's worthless. Can't understand how you ever made it back with an engine like that."

On September 29, MK sent me to McGrath and Bethel in the old Pilgrim that almost put me down in the Northway swamp.

Slim, meanwhile, had done such an outstanding job on defense construction that the military made him a full colonel and gave him a key command in the Aleutians. I hated to see Slim leave and I would miss him.

After a year and a month of memorable service, my own career with MK was drawing to a close, and a dream I'd cherished for years was about to become reality.

28

A DREAM FULFILLED

RUSS SORKNESS, a Northwest Airlines pilot, got me aside in the lobby of the Westward Hotel in Anchorage one evening.

"Northwest's hurting bad for pilots," he told me, "and they've got their eyes on you."

"You're kidding," I said. "How did Northwest ever hear about me?"

"I told them," he said, smiling.

I was stunned. The fact that I might actually qualify to fly transports and passenger planes for a nationwide airline was just mind-boggling.

"What do I do?"

"You deadhead down to Minneapolis on Northwest the first chance you get. You talk to Don King, NWA's chief pilot. If he gives you the nod and Mayo Clinic gives you a clean bill of health, you're hired. Take my word for it."

"Thanks, Russ," I said.

"Don't thank me, Herm. We need you desperately. We're getting pooped from all those extra flights."

I passed muster with Don King and with Mayo. After that the red carpet was rolled out for me at Northwest's general offices in Minneapolis, where I was photographed, fingerprinted and closely interrogated by a clean-cut young attorney who wanted to know whether I was a Communist.

I gave my not-too-reluctant goodbyes to the fine people at MK.

139

My NWA training began December 24, 1942. I was put through the paces by dedicated, no-nonsense instructors. I spent endless hours in a Link Trainer that simulated the problems a pilot might encounter in a DC-3.

I got to know the DC-3 inside out. I learned to fly it under virtually all kinds of conditions — crosswind, downwind, no flaps, engine out, on fire — you name it. I never worked and studied harder nor concentrated so intensely.

The last hurdle confronted me on March 6, 1943 — a rigorous, no-holds-barred flight check under the eagle-eyed surveillance of the chief pilot at NWA's Billings, Montana, training school, Earl Hale. Hale, a meticulous, demanding man, didn't miss a thing I did throughout that crucial flight. He took careful note of every action and reaction, remaining disturbingly silent and noncommittal from start to finish, except for commands. By the time we landed I was all wrung out, tense and afraid I'd flunked. After we landed, Hale turned to me grinning and shook my hand.

"Damn fine ride, Lerdahl," he said. "You're in. I'm treating you to a steak tonight at the Northern to celebrate."

I was overjoyed. An airline pilot at last! I considered it an incredible triumph when I thought about that long, uncertain road I had come down since that first flight with Noel Wien. '

Earl and I were finishing dinner beneath glittering chandeliers when I was paged by a Northern bellboy.

The telephone call was from Ray Shinn at MK's Seattle office.

"Congratulations, Herm," were his first words.

"What on earth for, Ray?"

"You're a Northwest captain now, aren't you?"

"Sure, but how did you know? My final flight check was just a couple of hours ago."

I heard him chuckle. "We knew right away, Herm. MK has agents all over the place. Besides wanting to congratulate you, I'm calling to let you know we'd like you to come back to work for us. MK has just landed a big job in China. We're buying a brand-new, four-engine DC-4 that you'd be flying. Salary? You can just about name it. I can assure you, Herm, that after about ten years with us you'll be able to retire without financial worries for the rest of your life."

"Let me think it over, Ray," I said. "I'm flattered by your

offer and glad to know I didn't burn any bridges. If you don't hear from me some time tomorrow, you'll know my decision. Thanks."

"Whatever you decide, Herm, MK wishes you the very best."

After some thought, I realized I just couldn't leave NWA after they had given me the opportunity of a lifetime.

Northwest was the civilian contractor for the Army's Air Transport Command. Northwest pilots were considered officers of the Armed Forces, and under the Geneva Convention would be treated as such if they were unfortunate enough to become prisoners of war.

As a full-fledged NWA pilot, I took on a snappy new look. Wartime airline uniforms were indistinguishable from those of military officers — dark brown trousers and jackets, light shirts, black ties and black shoes. Topping it all off were gleaming captain's bars and wings of dark bronze.

The first time I wore the crisp new uniform, sixteen-year-old Herm junior proudly dropped by the hangar with a troop of his fellow Civil Air Patrol cadets. I had just stepped outside the door when they came marching by in perfect cadence and halted directly in front of me. Standing at attention, they snapped rigid salutes. Startled, I did nothing at first, wondering why my son was getting so red-faced. Then, the electric light switched on and I returned the kids' salute, to be rewarded by smiles from all of them.

Not long afterward, in Edmonton, three Canadian soldiers saluted me smartly and got it promptly returned, thanks to my being forewarned by the Civil Air Patrol cadets. NWA had briefed us on how to wear the uniform and how to behave in public (don't go anywhere you wouldn't take your mother), but nothing had been mentioned about saluting.

On March 15, 1943, NWA transferred me to Edmonton. I moved into the McDonald Hotel, two floors of which were occupied by NWA flight crews.

We were paid from $750 to $900 a month, depending upon our hours, and allowed a maximum of eighty-five flying hours a month. We flew the powerful — for those days — 2,250-horsepower DC-3s. We flew the twin-engine planes day and night in all kinds of weather, observing the legal minimums on which we had trained: four-hundred-foot ceiling and a mile visibility.

NWA flights out of Edmonton shuttled regularly to Fort St. John, Fort Nelson, Watson Lake and Whitehorse. I flew numerous schedules to Northway and Fairbanks.

In Fairbanks, I would check in at the old Nordale Hotel. Invariably I would run into someone I knew. It was good to chat with old friends I'd flown into or out of the bush. I enjoyed shooting the breeze with bush pilots still in the business. Everyone seemed happy to see me in my captain's uniform doing my thing for the war effort.

Between flights, reading detective stories was a marvelous escape. I'd sprawl out on the bed and plow through stacks of the shoot-'em-up pulps, sometimes dropping off to sleep in the middle of an exciting story. When I woke up, I'd read some more.

At Fairbanks I got my first glimpse of Russian pilots who ferried heavily loaded Lend-Lease aircraft to the Russian-German front. These pilots had a reputation for recklessness. For example, the Russians thought nothing of taking off from Fairbanks or Nome in DC-3s loaded down with 30,000 pounds or more when the load limit was 27,500.

On May 24, 1943, I deadheaded from Edmonton back to Minneapolis to begin training in the C-46, a twin-engine ship about twice the size of the DC-3. After successful completion of the training, I became NWA's C-46 flight instructor at Billings.

The position promised a little stability and I purchased a two-bedroom house with garage on Ash Street for sixty-two hundred dollars. Herm junior, sixteen at the time, attended high school in Billings and Robert, our second son who was then five, started school there. Herm began taking flying lessons from Al Gillis. He soloed in a Piper Cub and made a few cross-country trips, doing a good job of flying. I was disappointed he didn't keep it up — he would have made a fine NWA pilot.

Nellis Air Force Base at Reno began sending us their fighter pilots to be trained as transport pilots. When the young lieutenants gathered around to begin their training, I told them to forget all about rank and military protocol.

"I'm here to teach you to fly Army transports day and night under all kinds of conditions. Just call me Herm and we'll get along fine."

At the conclusion of one class, one of the lieutenants got me aside to let me in on a secret the young officers shared. "When we first laid eyes on you," he said, "we figured you were going to be a tough, mean S.O.B. We were prepared not to like you a damn bit. We want you to know we were wrong. Not only have you done a great job as instructor, you're one hell of a guy."

Something like that can feed a man's ego for an awfully long time.

Nothing, I found, is permanent in the flying business, not even my comfortable eight-to-five instructor's existence at Billings.

In June 1944 I transferred to Anchorage to begin active flying for NWA out of that city, primarily to points on the Aleutian Chain. At the time there were about thirty Northwest crews based in either Anchorage, Edmonton or Adak, regularly flying the Chain.

I was already familiar, of course, with flying in the Aleutians as a result of my MK flying experience. But that was in light planes; now I'd be flying DC-3s. And I would be responsible for flying relatively large numbers of passengers, mostly military, and tons of APO mail.

I had no idea what a challenging — and sometimes harrowing — assignment I was getting.

29

HOSTILE SKY AT TANAGA

DEATH TOOK NO HOLIDAY that night over Tanaga in the Aleutians. Mercilessly it snuffed out the lives of several bomber pilots who were seeking, as we were, some place to land in a blind world of clouds and fog. Along with the doomed pilots, we floundered in that dread world, yearning for a light, a sign, a miracle that might keep us among the living.

We were on a trip from Adak to Amchitka, Shemya and Attu on July 2, 1944. Ramon (Litz) Litzenberger was my co-pilot.

We broke through a ragged overcast on our approach to Amchitka, a long, narrow skeleton of an island with a volcano perched on one end. Despite half-mile visibility, we got down at Amchitka all right. Then, after refueling and cargo operations and adding a couple of passengers to the handful already aboard, we took off for Shemya. The weather reports we got were not good. Shemya was shrouded in thick, zero-zero fog and though we tried to get in twice, it was hopeless. On the last attempt I called for full takeoff power, got the gear and flaps up again, and began climbing steadily through the puddinglike fog. At twenty-five hundred, I cleaned up the airplane to cruise configuration.

Litz called Attu for a clearance to Massacre Bay airfield thirty-five miles from Shemya. Army air traffic control suggested we hold south of the Attu range station at three thousand until further notice. "Other traffic in the area," they told us.

Other traffic? In this pea soup?

We saw the "other traffic" in a moment. Two Lockheed

Ventura bombers popped out of the solid overcast to the west like a couple of silvery fish breaking free from a dark ocean. The planes continued to climb vertically not more than five hundred feet in front of us.

"Hey," I admonished approach control, "we got bombers coming out of the woodwork up here — what's the cotton-picking deal?"

"Sorry," the controller came back, his voice tense and at the edge of exasperation. "Those boys are lost after a mission and trying to find their way back to our field."

I felt sheepish about wising off, but now became uneasy about our own situation.

After a decent pause I asked, "Any chance things might open up down there? Any idea how much longer we're gonna have to hold for clearance?"

"Stand by."

With more than half our fuel supply gone and dusk setting in, we were up against it. Glumly I watched a blood-red sun get swallowed in the murk.

The radio crackled and the Northwest dispatcher at Adak came on. "Weather's lousy everywhere," he said. "Tanaga's the only place open. Suggest you consider trying to get in there."

"How about Attu?"

"Out of the question."

Moments later, to our surprise, Attu radio came on to tell us, "You're cleared to land — number one for approach."

We made a left procedure turn, putting us four hundred feet over the water, heading north.

"Weather here closing in fast . . ." Attu tower warned.

I was down to sixty feet above the water and could see no break in the fog — no lights, nothing. I gave up, calling for gear up and full power.

Now we were in a right climbing turn at two hundred feet. I called for flaps up. At five hundred, I called for climb power. My decision was to hightail it to Tanaga, the only escape hatch left.

The Northwest dispatcher at Adak told us what we already knew. "All stations except Tanaga socked in tight as a drum," he reported gloomily. By throttling back, we might have about an hour of fuel remaining after flying the four hundred miles to Tanaga.

En route, Adak operations kept us posted on Tanaga's weather. Mercifully, it clung at a two-hundred-foot ceiling and one-mile visibility, but I knew it could close at any time. There was a good likelihood we might end up trapped above the fog. What then? I didn't want to think about it.

I tried to shake off a sense of doom as we monitored transmissions between the Ventura bomber pilots and Shemya tower.

The last poignant exchange came as we were passing Amchitka. I felt admiration for the Army pilot, whose voice reflected not terror but annoyance that death was overtaking him in this way. "If I can't see the runway on the next pass, we've gotta bail out somewhere," he said calmly. Then, after a long pause: "So long, everybody." There were no further transmissions. Just the silence of death.

We started our descent in lousy weather thirty miles southwest of Tanaga, seeing nothing but tomblike corridors of fog in an unreal, dark world void of reference points. I prayed we'd spot something when we got just a couple of miles out, but at that position there was no hint of any kind of light below, no bright, lifesaving blemish that might offer salvation.

My palms and forehead were wet with perspiration and the band of my cap felt clammy with dampness. My eyes strained. No forward visibility at all — just dark, shifting draperies of cloud and fog. I glanced at Litz, who looked cool, professional. "See anything, Litz?" I asked.

"Nothing." His voice sounded distant and hollow over the steady drone of the engines.

Seven miles from Tanaga — not a glimmer.

Six miles.

Five miles. Hallelujah! A tiny, bluish pinpoint of light broke the graveyard fogginess ahead.

"Good old Bartows," Litz yelled, grinning.

Tanaga's main runway was bracketed by twin rows of high-intensity Bartow lights. I felt a surge of gratitude toward the guy who invented them, and to those who installed them here in the bleak Aleutians.

Skimming over the airport at two hundred, the god-sent Bartows paraded past like bright blue blossoms drifting in a dark lake.

Even though we had a fix on the runway, we would be asking

for it if we attempted to go in without adequate visibility for landing. A good part of the runway had already been invaded by fog, which seemed to be advancing.

On my second approach try, I let the ship down to just above the water. From this position I could see the parallel lines of Bartows up ahead, but from a different, better angle. Two hundred feet from the runway and skimming the sea at forty feet, I called for full flaps.

Too low! I yanked back on the wheel to regain altitude. Now the lights stood out more clearly, providing intermittent glimpses of the runway.

I felt all kinds of misgivings. At best, it was a marginal landing situation. But there was no alternative: I had to go in.

I felt a sharp jolt as the gear touched the steel mat. The far end of the runway ahead of us was buried in fog that was now moving across the midsection of the field. We plowed into it, but our speed had tapered off and we were safe.

As we came to a halt, I removed my headset and cap. The sweat dammed up by my headband poured in thin rivulets down my face. I wiped the stuff off my cheeks with the back of my hand, unafraid now of the dense billows of fog that surrounded us and began snuffing out the Bartow lights. In less than ten minutes there was no visibility whatsoever on Tanaga. Had we arrived a few minutes later, a landing attempt would have been suicidal.

"Close call," I said to Litz as I ran a handkerchief around the inside of my damp collar.

He seemed surprised. "My first trip out this way, Herm," he said. "I thought this is what you guys go through all the time."

30

FAREWELL TO
FLYING COMRADES

DURING WHAT HAS aptly been referred to as "the thousand-mile war," the military made every effort to keep up the morale of the troops on those miserable appendages to Alaska. USO units regularly visited the camps, occasionally bringing stars like Bob Hope and Martha Raye. Joe Louis, the famed "Brown Bomber," was on one of my flights from Shemya to Attu.

Wearing the uniform of an Army sergeant, Joe visited all the major Aleutian bases, shaking hands with GIs and occasionally boxing anybody willing to enter the ring with him.

Joe was as excited as a kid when my co-pilot, Marv Davis, invited him to sit in the co-pilot's seat just before we got to Attu.

Joe's physique amazed me. His massive arms, fists and knuckles dwarfed mine. Yet he seemed like a kind, gentle, easygoing person.

Louis kept peering out, seeing nothing but thick clouds and driving rain. "How do you guys know where you're going when you can't see?" I offered a brief explanation.

Taxiing in to the operations building at Attu, I could see hundreds of GIs milling around in the freezing rain just to get a glimpse of Louis. Marv pulled the window back so the troops could see him sitting up front in the cockpit. After he got off, the troops literally carried him away.

■ ■ ■

Neither Marvin Davis nor I will ever forget our blind landing at Amchitka. Marv, my co-pilot for August and September 1944, had flown with me many times before, and we got along like bread and butter.

The slim, blond, almost six-foot pilot was born in Batavia, Illinois, and had played football at Eau Claire, Wisconsin. Marv was fifty-one numbers behind me on the NWA seniority list when he went to work for Northwest in September 1941.

We left Anchorage for Adak on August 8, 1944, making routine stops at Cold Bay and North Shore near Fort Glenn. The next morning we left Adak for Amchitka, Shemya and Attu.

Amchitka was reporting zero-zero conditions as we approached — no ceiling, no visibility. Though it didn't seem we had a prayer of landing, I advised the tower we were going to make a practice approach to check out the field's instrument landing system (ILS).

I connected with the ILS heading at fifteen hundred feet and followed its "beam" on in. At seven hundred, we could see the approach lights' dim yellow glow. Marv kept calling out airspeed and altitude as I descended. In moments the landing gear was down and the plane was in landing configuration.

At two hundred, as the ILS kept us in the groove for a landing, we could see two rows of runway lights, then at one hundred the yellow approach lights began swooping by, to be replaced instantly by the clear, glowing runway lights. I called for full flaps then went in, setting the plane down gently, taxiing past a faint blue light indicating a taxiway exit, and pulled off there, holding, since the area was now wrapped in deep fog.

The radio crackled. "Do you plan to proceed to Adak?" the military controller asked, thinking we were still aloft.

"Not immediately," Marv responded. "We're on the ground and holding at the first taxi exit. Can't see a thing. Can you send someone out to lead us in?"

I heard the controller gulp. Ten minutes later the base's "follow me" jeep arrived and led us toward operations, glancing back nervously from time to time as I tailgated him.

At base headquarters, a cheeky second lieutenant curtly informed me that "whether you like it or not, you're going to stay overnight at Amchitka."

"Why?" I asked.

"Regulations," he said. "We can't clear you out in weather like this."

Though I always tried to cultivate good relations with the military, this guy's arrogant attitude bugged me. "We'll make the decision on whether we stay or go," I said. "We're authorized. All your tower people are required to do is give us traffic advisories."

His face reddened with annoyance.

We loaded up with fuel and cargo and I signed a clearance, taking all responsibility. Using the directional gyro for steering and the Bartow lights for points of reference, we got out without any trouble and were back at Adak in less than two hours.

■ ■ ■

Marvin was back flying with me in November and December of 1944. On one mid-November trip to Adak, I was pleased, at our routine Naknek stop, to meet Major John Cross of Kotzebue, Naknek's new commanding officer.

At Cold Bay, Alaska's Governor Gruening and my old Holy Cross friend, Bishop Fitzgerald, joined us.

The bishop shook my hand warmly and said, "Now I can sleep all the way to Adak."

Approaching Dutch Harbor, a brilliant red rocket streaked across our flight path. The military was asking us to identify ourselves over our "friend or foe" transmitter. I responded promptly. We were told that if we crashed in enemy territory we were to activate the switch in the opposite direction to destroy the unit.

As we were signing in at the Atka mess hall, the tall, young corporal manning the desk glanced at my signature.

"Would you happen to know an Olaf Lerdahl of Cyrus, Minnesota?" he asked.

"My brother."

The young GI eagerly grasped my hand. "Man," he exclaimed, "I've been in Atka for almost two years and you're the first guy I've seen from home. Would you mind if I came over to your Quonset after chow to yak a bit?"

"Not at all — come on over," I said.

I was in my pajamas in bed, reading pulp detective stories, when the GI came in. I put my magazine aside as he pulled up a chair.

151

A Norwegian like myself, Luther Kirkevold was born and reared on a farm bordering Lake Minnewaska. I was born on a farm near Cyrus, Minnesota, in the same general vicinity.

"Remember," Luther asked eagerly, "how the Lerdahls and the Kirkevolds used to share the same hired man?"

"Sure do. Nels Hoium from Norway. He retired at our farm and died there."

"Remember the sixteen-foot-high pile of wood Nels chopped?" he asked. "There was a picture and story about it in the *Minneapolis Tribune.*"

"Yeah," I said. "Remember the big iceboat Nels built for us, with runners sixteen feet long. We used to whiz across the lake about a hundred miles an hour. . . ."

And so it went, far into the night, nostalgic talk about home folks and home places, so meaningful to this lonely GI stuck out on this bleak island.

Much as I enjoyed talking to Luther, I was exhausted after the long flight and unable to keep from nodding off. About the last thing I remember before I began my usual raucous snoring was, "Remember the big storm . . ." Luther returned the next morning and was waiting for me to wake up.

"Sorry I conked out on you last night, Luther," I told him, rubbing my eyes.

"That's okay," he said. "I saw you were real tired so I took off. But I wanted to talk some more before you left."

■ ■ ■

Johnny Woodhead, Northwest's director of flight operations in Minneapolis, and Don King, Edmonton operations manager, were my passengers on a DC-3 flight from Adak to Shemya in June 1945. Bored with his desk job, Woodhead asked to fly the plane on the Adak-Shemya leg with King as his co-pilot. I agreed.

At the time Shemya was a gigantic Aleutian military base. More than twenty-eight thousand GIs were stationed there to repel the expected enemy assault. The base had four huge light plants, several massive hangars, three large mess halls and a forest of GI-filled Quonset huts scattered across the tundra. The place bristled with planes, guns and other armament — a huge military "city" on the bleak tundra that had once been home to only a handful of Aleuts.

After chow, from our perch in the cockpit of our DC-3, Woodhead and I watched the stream of P-40s swarming in and out of the base.

We observed the last P-40 in a flight of five drift off to the left and touch down on the parking strip, about one hundred fifty feet to our right. As the plane's wheels struck ground the landing gear shocks bottomed out, bouncing the aircraft off the steel mats and back into the air, where the pilot fought to bring it under control.

I watched in horror as the plane's big, long propeller blade, glinting in the afternoon sun, zoomed toward us as we sat frozen in the cockpit seats. I figured that even if the prop didn't kill us, one of those retracting wheels would come smashing through the cabin. Scrambling to get out, Woodhead and I found ourselves wedged against each other in the companionway door. We expected to hear the fighter collide with the DC-3 at any moment, but the pilot managed to coax a few more inches of altitude out of his roaring P-40. We watched in frozen fascination. It was so close we could see the cotter pins in the bolts on the gear as the undersection of the plane swooped past.

"Another coat of paint — " Woodhead groaned.

■ ■ ■

My co-pilot on that fateful evening in October 1944 was Doc Salisbury, who'd gone through check-out school with me in Billings.

We had intended to leave Adak for Anchorage at 9:30 P.M. but a fast-developing Aleutian storm convinced us otherwise. By the time I filled out our flight plan, wind velocity outside exceeded fifty-five miles an hour. Even so, Doc and I figured we might be able to beat the storm out of Adak, so we scooted over to the plane, started it and taxied down to the far south end of the runway.

Doc held the wheel firmly while I struggled to keep the ship from blowing off the taxiway. A fierce crosswind was causing us to sashay badly. Heavy wind gusts wrenched and tossed the ship as though it were a toy. Repeatedly the wind lifted the plane right off the shocks and slammed it down again.

All this disturbed me more than I wanted Doc to know. As I held near the end of the runway, we monitored the exchange between traffic control and "Bubs" Christian, the pilot of an incoming NWA

153

flight. As Christian began his approach to Adak from the west, we heard the tower supplying weather, including the ominous announcement that winds had reached ninety miles an hour.

A savage wind gust hit our plane, tilting it until it creaked and groaned.

Doc was looking pale and queasy. I looked over at him and tried to grin. "You know, Doc," I said, "you can go ahead and call me a coward, but I haven't got the guts to take off in this kind of crosswind."

"Make that two cowards, Herm," Doc said, looking relieved.

Gusts battered our plane all the way back to the ramp.

As we were heading back we heard the tower repeatedly calling the number of Bubs's ship. There was no response. I felt weak and sick in the pit of my stomach. With the wind so terrible here on the ground, what was it like up there, inside Bubs's plane?

I strained to hear any response to traffic control's repeated calls, praying the silence was because Bubs was just too busy flying through that awful wind to respond.

Though we canceled our flight plan and prepared to remain overnight, we wouldn't budge from the dispatcher's counter. We had to wait — no matter how long it took — for word about Bubs's plane.

Twenty minutes later the military police called to say they were checking out a report that a plume of flame had been spotted on nearby Mount Moffett.

I was stunned. Much as I didn't want to accept it, the grim reality couldn't be ignored. Bubs had crashed. All I could do was hope that some miracle had spared the two crewmen and eighteen passengers.

The door suddenly whipped open and Walt Edwards, NWA's manager at Adak, struggled to shut it as the howling wind insisted on keeping it open.

When he got the door closed, Walt stormed up to us. "What's the matter, Herm?" he blustered. "Why aren't you on your way to Anchorage?"

I didn't respond.

"They need your ship badly in Anchorage. They — "

Suddenly he noted the dead silence and the somber faces.

"It's Bubs," I said. "Long overdue. Fire's been spotted on Moffett."

"Oh, my God," Walt exclaimed.

About an hour later, military police reported by radio from the mountain that they had reached the scene and wreckage of the silver-and-red DC-3 was scattered widely along the slope.

"Any survivors?" the dispatcher asked anxiously.

"None."

I thought a lot about Bubs as we flew back to Anchorage the next day. He was in my thoughts as we skirted the bleak landscape of Attu, where bloody battles had been fought to wrest the island from the Japanese. I thought of him as we passed over the wreck of a C-47 on the side of an Aleutian hill. The plane's fuselage had cracked in half. I thought of him as we flew over the remains of a twin-engine Douglas bomber being pounded to pieces by the foaming, icy surf.

I thought of the days when Bubs and I had gone to check-out school together in Billings. He had been my co-pilot during my first ninety days with NWA.

And I thought of all the other fine NWA crews who died in the line of duty over the years since I had begun flying with the line. John Hart and Kenney Jones died near Watson Lake airport in January 1944. Ray Propstel and Pete Bliven were killed in a crash near Mount McKinley in October 1944. Gil Enger and Ray Venderbush vanished without a trace in August 1943 on a flight from Fairbanks to Edmonton.

They and all the others brought me a deep sense of loss and grief.

As my plane flew toward Anchorage across the gray and lonely Aleutians, I saluted them all. I mourned the loss of Bubs and the others with the sorrow I would feel in the death of a brother.

31

FLYING THE UNFLYABLE

FLYING A CRIPPLED passenger liner in a wild Aleutian storm
was never touched on in those endless NWA training sessions aimed
at preparing pilots for just about any emergency.

On that terrible flight in late January 1945, the insufferable
Aleutian weather kept getting worse. I had flown the Chain night and
day for more than eleven hundred flying hours over thirteen months,
and I couldn't remember a single day on which you could call the
weather good. On this traumatic flight, it was particularly bad.

Besides coping with the weather, I was forced to make a decision affecting the course of my co-pilot's life — the hardest decision I
ever had to make in my career with NWA.

My co-pilot on that particular flight, an outstanding pilot
I'll call Jack, was a personable, dedicated man who, like me, had
always dreamed of a career as a commercial pilot. He started out
with Northwest as a Link Trainer operator, then won a slot as
co-pilot.

Jack was of medium height, with dark eyes and dark brown
hair neatly slicked back. His keen intelligence, remarkable vocabulary
and winning personality would have won him success in just about
anything he put his mind to. As it turned out, had I done things by the
book, that probably would have been Jack's last flight. To have
deprived Jack of flying would have broken his heart, just as it would
have broken mine.

I was braced for horrible weather when we left Anchorage at
eight in the evening, with eight military passengers occupying the

DC-3's twin rows of bucket seats. The cargo included a couple of dozen bulging sacks of APO mail.

Before our departure we were told that a storm front with high-velocity winds was sweeping up the Chain. I knew that winds of a hundred miles an hour were not uncommon. In one storm, gusts of 137 miles an hour shattered the anemometer at Shemya, rolling up steel runway mats like carpets, ripping off roofs and sending windows, lumber and shingles whizzing through the air.

When such devastating winds hit an aircraft while aloft, a pilot has a real fight on his hands. Longtime Aleutian pilots soon become acquainted with stomach-wrenching plunges known as sinkers. These "air pockets" can send you plummeting downward several hundred feet, even though the plane's engines are droning away at full climb power. When you hit bottom, it's like an express elevator smashing into the bottom of a shaft. The resulting spine-twisting jolt shakes you to your teeth and jerks your chin down to your chest. Then you begin whizzing back up in the "fast elevator," just as speedily and just as uncontrollably.

I felt absolutely powerless against those savage "uppers" and "downers." They converted the plane into a kind of yo-yo being manipulated by giant, irresistible forces. Often I'd brace my arm against something solid to keep my head from smashing against the left window. Meanwhile, I'd struggle to keep the plane right side up and moving in the right general direction.

I often wondered how the plane's wings could withstand such punishment. Occasionally, almost as if to reassure myself that they remained attached, I'd switch on the wing de-icing lights and peer out across those slender, pliant surfaces that protected us from death on the rocks or sea below. With fascination I'd watch the wings dance and tremble in the faint glow of the lights. I'd marvel at how they kept shaping and reshaping themselves from concave to convex, their incredible strength and flexibility withstanding heavy punishment.

On this night, Jack seemed nonplussed by the nasty weather we began hitting as we approached Fort Glenn. After torrents of hail and intermittent squalls, we encountered a spectacular "downer" and "upper."

As we groped our way down through curtains of hail, rain and snow toward the runway threshold, fog kept us from seeing the runway. I asked Jack to contact the tower and ask the controller to blink the runway lights a couple of times. Instantly, twin rows of bright splotches emerged in the fog ahead.

We now had the field in sight and were promptly cleared for our approach. We went in at 1:30 A.M., fighting the wind all the way to the ground and even after we got on the ground. Once stopped, we didn't dare turn the ship. It was being pounded by hammer blows so intense that rivets were creaking.

"We need help out here," Jack told the tower tersely.

"Help's on the way," the operator assured us. In a few minutes, two heavy steel-tracked vehicles clanked over to where we were parked. GI crews anchored the plane's wings to the vehicles, then installed blocks for the ailerons, elevator and rudder.

A couple of passengers deplaned down the aluminum steps. Jack and I followed, bending low against the wind as we fought our way to the mess hall. While we tarried over sandwiches and coffee, ground crews braved the lashing winds to refuel the plane and transfer cargo. Six Adak passengers reboarded for the continuation of their flight.

"Like to fly 'er to Adak?" I asked Jack when we returned to the cockpit.

"Sure," he said. Jack had flown "left seat" with me a couple of times before and had earned my full confidence.

The storm's violence set the stage for what happened next. When the ground crew signaled that the control blocks were coming off, both of us were preoccupied with the battering the wind was giving us. I retrieved my headset and transferred it to the right side, while Jack took my seat and began running up the engines. We went through the takeoff checklist, still preoccupied with the pitching and rocking of the ship in the rising wind.

The tower cleared us for takeoff to Adak, and Jack soon had us climbing out to three thousand feet on an eastward heading. He then turned the plane west, continuing to climb until we reached eight thousand. There, Jack very competently set up the cockpit for cruise.

Propelled by a strong tail wind, we went whistling by Fort Glenn through dense sleet, snow, rain and hail. Though everything appeared relatively normal, we were, in fact, brushing the edge of disaster.

The weather kept deteriorating as we approached Adak. We had a ragged four-hundred-foot ceiling and less than three-quarters of a mile visibility.

Beyond our Great Sitkin navigational "fix," Jack startled me by turning to me abruptly and saying: "Herm, I'd just as soon you'd take over for the Adak let-down."

I stared at him in disbelief. Was it a matter of confidence? "Naw, you go ahead, Jack," I protested. "Adak'll be a breeze for you — you're a whiz on instruments."

Jack was adamant. "No — no, Herm," he insisted. "I just don't feel up to it now." He put the plane on automatic pilot, abruptly yanked off the headset and mike, and stepped into the companionway.

Silently we traded seats. I plugged in my set, still puzzled by his insistence on the switch.

With the approach to Adak dead ahead, I unplugged auto pilot and prepared to hand-fly. Wiggling the controls to make sure we were clear of auto pilot, I was puzzled by the strange, sluggish reaction.

Quickly I unfastened my seat belt, stood up and switched on the wing de-icer lights. Then I leaned over to peer out across the wing, my head in front of Jack's face. What I saw hit with icy shock.

Oh, God — no! No! I thought.

The bright white-and-orange-checkered aileron block with the rubber bungee cord still in place was still clinging to the wing. Now it was a deadly time bomb, robbing us of aileron control. With the ailerons blocked like that, a safe landing would be almost impossible, especially in the turbulence we were experiencing.

Jack's routine pre-takeoff checks should have assured that the block had been removed. There was no doubt about it — the damn thing was still out there and we were in for it.

I was scared.

Silently I returned to my seat, fastened my seat belt, and switched the wing lights off. Should I tell Jack? All that would do, I concluded, would be to get him as thoroughly upset as I was. And it might shake him up even more because, as pilot in command, his had been the primary responsibility for assuring that the ailerons and other controls were fully operational. So for the time being I said nothing. I concentrated on trying to figure out how, without ailerons, I was going to maneuver the plane for the tricky landing at Adak.

Jack kept staring at me quizzically as I corrected the plane's heading by pushing hard on the left rudder, skidding the plane into a left bank and turn to begin my descent to the Adak runway. To halt the turn I applied right rudder, again skidding the plane and unmercifully jolting our passengers. Those shallow bucket seats behind us were designed for troop transport, not aileronless flight in an Aleutian storm.

While I managed to maintain a fairly good, though zigzagging approach, Jack kept eyeing me oddly, no doubt wondering what had got into me to be flying so erratically.

Approaching Adak's runway, we pierced banks of ragged clouds. All the way down we were lashed by a torrential downpour that converted the windshield into shifting opaqueness. That glaze was all I needed at a time when I had to figure out how I was going to get an aileronless DC-3 around to the south end of the runway, then turn it 180 degrees for the approach. Those badly overworked rudders, I decided, would have to get me in somehow.

Southbound now and down to a hundred feet, I paralleled the runway, moving downwind and well to the right to maintain a clear view of the Bartow lights sweeping past to my left.

Gear down, flaps set for landing, I jammed left rudder hard, bringing the left wing down in a very steep sixty-degree left turn. Then I reversed rudder and elevators and coordinated the two, pulling back sharply on the wheel to swing around to the required north heading. Elevators and right rudder brought the left wing back up sharply, again jostling and maybe scaring hell out of the passengers. Repeatedly I applied rudder to get the wings leveled off as we approached the runway through dense sheets of rain and intermittent curtains of fog.

I called for full flaps and put the plane down near the middle of the runway. As we continued our landing roll, my mind wrestled with what I was going to do once we came to a halt.

I knew that the moment our mechanics spotted that block on the wing, a tortuous process would be set in motion that would reverberate all the way to Minneapolis. There would be investigations, interrogations, lengthy reports and, ultimately, serious repercussions, especially for Jack.

According to the manual, it was my duty now to prepare a full, detailed report of the incident. I was taught to live by the manual always and without question. Yet, the manual notwithstanding, I felt reluctant to take a step that might wipe out a fine pilot's career all because of a once-in-a-lifetime goof, a freak oversight that would never happen again, especially to Jack. At the same time, I instinctively rebelled at sweeping something so serious under the rug. A seesaw battle raged within me before I was able to make a conscience-wrenching decision.

Instead of taxiing over to operations as I normally would, I headed the plane toward the north end of the runway. As we moved slowly along, I leaned over and yelled to Jack: "Listen carefully. Even before we stop, get out in the companionway, fast. Get your coat on, go over to the door and get somebody to help you hold it open. Put the steps in place, climb down, then scoot under the airplane to the trailing edge of the right wing. Quickly remove the shock cord and aileron block from the wing. Hide the cord and block under your coat, then hightail it back here as fast as you can. Retrieve the steps and close the door. After that, we'll get going again. If anybody asks what you're up to, don't answer. Pretend you didn't hear."

Blood drained from Jack's face as the full awareness of what had happened struck him. Without a word he got to his feet, prepared to do as I had instructed.

Deception wasn't going to be easy. NWA operations people, I knew, were wondering at this moment why I wasn't coming in. And I knew the tower had the glasses on us as we remained mysteriously parked more than a quarter of a mile from where we should have been. Very soon they would begin asking questions. I didn't have to wait long.

The radio crackled: "Lerdahl, you in some kind of trouble out there?" the controller wanted to know.

Now that I had plunged off the diving board, the outrageous white lie came easily. "Uh — no trouble at all," I managed. "We just spotted a man — or maybe it was a bear — cutting across the runway in front of us. Thought we'd stop a bit to make sure the runway was clear."

"A man or bear out on the runway? Can't be!"

"I know it sounds impossible, but we saw something."

There was a long pause. Then the controller asked: "Well,

isn't whoever or whatever you saw out of the way by now? Any reason you can't taxi in?"

"No reason at all," I said. "Be there in a jiffy. Excuse the delay."

Jack came rushing back, ghostly pale, panting from his wild dash under the plane. Bulging beneath his tunic was the blankety-blank block.

"Anybody ask you what's going on, Jack?"

"No, Herm," he said, still highly agitated, "but everybody was staring and wondering what in hell I was running out there for."

I hid the block as the ground crew directed us in, and when we were on the ramp I shut the engines down. I hung on in the cockpit with Jack long after the passengers got off — I didn't want to run into anybody who might ask questions.

At operations, I got questions. An NWA mechanic dashed over as I was turning in my papers. "What delayed you?" he asked. "Why didn't you come straight in? Some trouble?"

"No trouble at all," I explained as calmly as I could, noting that a couple of off-duty NWA pilots standing nearby had inter-rupted their own conversation to eavesdrop.

The mechanic grinned. "Glad it was nothing serious," he said.

It was almost four in the morning. After a bite to eat at the all-night mess hall, Jack and I wordlessly battled the wind to the nearby Bachelor Quarters in two end-to-end Quonsets.

I had no inkling of the devastating effect the night's incident was having on Jack until he slumped on his bunk across from me, his body twisted in an odd half-sitting, half-lying position. He looked crushed and full of despair.

"Okay, Jack — out with it. What in hell's the matter?"

"*You* tell *me*," he said, anguish in his voice. "I'm going to get fired — isn't that right? Fired for that goddamn, lousy, stupid mis-take!" He smashed his fist repeatedly into his pillow. "I *deserve* to get fired for dropping the ball like that."

"Hey, stop punishing yourself, Jack," I told him quietly. "You're not getting fired. I think you've learned your lesson, and you will never take off again without first making sure everything's func-tioning properly, as we were trained to do. If I'd been on my toes, I might have caught it before we got off the ground. Anyway, it's over with, done. I'm closing the book on the whole thing as of now."

I began unbuttoning my shirt. "One last thing," I told him, "nothing has changed my confidence in you. As far as I'm concerned, you're still a good, dedicated, conscientious pilot. I'll be happy to fly with you anytime."

Jack walked over and gripped my hand. "Thanks, Herm," he said.

It was the only time in my career I ever compromised pilot discipline and going by the book. I never regretted that decision. Jack's unblemished record of fine service to NWA in the years then ahead, I feel, fully vindicated the forbidden action I took.

32

FAREWELL TO ALASKA

ON AUGUST 6, 1945, I was driving from Billings to Sweet Grass on the Canadian border, on my way back to Edmonton after a short stay at home.

Approaching Great Falls, I heard the shattering news flash about the dropping of the atomic bomb on Hiroshima. And on August 15, on an NWA flight from Fairbanks to Edmonton, I heard the exciting news of the enemy surrender and the arrival of VJ Day.

The driver of the jeep taking me and my co-pilot from the Edmonton airport to the McDonald Hotel downtown turned to us and said, "Wait till you see the city — it's a madhouse!"

He was right. It took us more than an hour to move through downtown streets to our hotel. Wildly celebrating crowds jammed the streets. Canadian and U.S. flags were everywhere. Buses and streetcars were immobilized in the milling crowds. It seemed that every man, woman and child in Edmonton was in the center of the city that day. When we finally got to the hotel, we found the lobby packed with people. We went to our room, freshened up and came down to the dining room. We had no intention of venturing out into that mob on the street.

Tired, I went to bed early, still hearing the muffled roar sent up by thousands of excited, cheering celebrants outside. Around two in the morning the celebration was still in full swing, and all I could see from my hotel window was a solid, seething mass of milling, yelling people.

The next morning, as we walked down to the Shasta Cafe for

breakfast, cleanup crews were busily hauling away tons of debris left on the streets.

The war was over.

Very shortly I was saying farewell to Alaska. My new assignment was flying GIs from their ports of disembarkation back to their home areas. Instead of Adak, Atka and Cold Bay, I was now shuttling between America's great cities — New York, Chicago, Milwaukee, Minneapolis and Seattle.

So many years had drifted by since I first discovered the joy of flying, during that brief hop with Noel Wien. The years couldn't have been better to me as a veteran pilot with one of the world's great airlines.

I never lost my sense of awe and respect for the wonders of the modern commercial airline environment I had become a part of — the safety, the speed, the superb personnel, the up-to-the-minute equipment.

Many times I thanked fate for laying the groundwork for all this. None of it would have been possible without that meeting with Noel Wien, the fifty-five hundred hours of Alaska bush flying, and the job with MK that followed.

Ever since, Alaska has been a part of me. High over the Midwest on a winter night, I'd be enjoying the sight of glittering patches of light that were the communities of America on the great prairie. And occasionally I'd see in the dark, velvet sky, shifting ribbons and tassels of color that instantly recalled memories of Alaska.

It was during one of those flights that I decided to preserve those memories by writing this book.

In many ways, I have never left Alaska. The Great Land remains in my mind, wherever I go.

To the end.

EPILOGUE

HERMAN I. LERDAHL, who was born on February 26, 1906, on a farm near Cyrus, Minnesota, died on January 15, 1983, at the Desert Hospital, Palm Springs, California.

Survivors included his wife, Daisy, and his two sons, Herman junior and Robert.

Among his effects was the manuscript on which this book is based.

ACKNOWLEDGMENTS

I AM GRATEFUL TO Daisy Lerdahl for her patience and under-standing during the many months when this book was being produced.

I am especially indebted to Ethel Dassow, Senior Book Editor for Alaska Northwest Books at the time this book was being written. Without her guidance and perceptive suggestions the book would not have been possible.

For photos contained in this book I am deeply grateful for the help provided by Daisy Lerdahl, Herman Lerdahl, Jr., Morrison-Knudsen Co., Alaskan Air Command historian John Cloe, and the National Park Service.

I received technical advice from two experts: Ted Spencer, Director of the Alaska Aviation Heritage Museum, the Alaska authority on vintage aircraft; and John Underwood, of California. I am grateful for their helpful suggestions.

ABOUT THE WRITER

CLIFF CERNICK IS A PIONEER Alaska newspaper reporter and editor. A graduate of the University of Washington (he's from Cle Elum, Washington), Cernick was one of the first editors of *The Anchorage Daily News*, now Alaska's largest newspaper, and also was the editor of *The Fairbanks Daily News-Miner*. For more than twenty years before his retirement in 1983, Cernick was Public Affairs Officer for the Federal Aviation Administration in Washington, D.C., Los Angeles, Seattle and Anchorage. In addition to coauthoring *Skystruck*, Cernick helped edit *Winging It!*, the story of Jack Jefford, pioneer Alaska aviator.

If you enjoyed the flying adventures of Herm Lerdahl in Skystruck, *we have more books about the legendary bush pilots of the North:*

WINGING IT!

Jack Jefford, pioneer Alaskan aviator, tells his own story: the most thrilling, amusing, and heartwarming experiences of a "pilot's pilot" who flew everything from biplanes to jets. Edited by Carmen Jefford Fisher and Mark Fisher, with Cliff Cernick.
322 pages, paperback, $12.95 ($15.95 Canadian), ISBN 0-88240-371-0

ERNIE BOFFA: *Canadian Bush Pilot*

Florence Whyard tells the story of pioneer bush pilot Ernie Boffa's heroic flying in the North country.
141 pages, paperback, $7.95 ($9.95 Canadian), ISBN 0-88240-264-1

FRANK BARR: *Bush Pilot in Alaska and the Yukon*

Dermot Cole recounts the life of Frank Barr, legendary aviator. Barr was known for surviving forced landings and repairing wrecked planes and flying them out after being stranded in the bush for weeks.
115 pages, paperback, $7.95 ($9.95 Canadian), ISBN 0-88240-314-1

Ask for these books at your favorite bookstore, or contact Alaska Northwest Books™ for a complete catalog.

Alaska Northwest Books™

A division of GTE Discovery Publications, Inc.
P.O. Box 3007
Bothell, WA 98041-3007
1-800-343-4567